D1103924

Academic Libraries and Training

**FOUNDATIONS IN LIBRARY AND
INFORMATION SCIENCE, Volume 29**

Editors: Thomas W. Leonhardt, *Dean, University Libraries, W.M. Know
Memorial Library, University of the Pacific*

                Murray S. Martin, *University Librarian and Professor of Library
Science Emeritus, Tufts University*

Academic
Libraries
and Training

Editor: MARYRUTH PHELPS GLOGOWSKI

Interim Director
E.H. Butler Library
Buffalo State College
State University of New York

 **JAI PRESS INC.**

Greenwich, Connecticut   *London, England*

Library of Congress Cataloging-in-Publication Data

Academic libraries and training / editor. Maryruth Phelps Glogowski.
     p.   cm.—(Foundations in library and information science;
  v. 29)
    Includes index.
    ISBN 1-55938-598-7
    1. Academic libraries—United States. 2. Library employees—
Training of—United States. I. Glogowski, Maryruth. II. Series.
  Z675.U5A332 1994
  027.7'0973—dc20

                                     94-37215
                                        CIP

ISBN: 1-55938-598-7

Library of Congress Catalogue Number: 94-37215

Manufactured in the United States of America

FOUNDATIONS IN LIBRARY AND INFORMATION SCIENCE
A Series of Monographs, Texts and Treatises

Edited by
Thomas W. Leonhardt
Holt Library, University of the Pacific

and
Murray S. Martin
University Librarian and Professor of Library Science Emeritus,
Tufts University

CONTENTS

ACKNOWLEDGMENTS

My thanks go to the *Foundations in Library and Information Science* series editor, Murray Martin, who entrusted this project to me and Susan Oppenheim of JAI Press who was so patient and helpful. A sincere acknowledgment goes to my terrific former library director, Dr. George Charles Newman, for his positive attitude, motivation, good ideas, and for providing a truly supportive scholarly atmosphere. Thanks go to my wonderful secretary, Kathy Babcock, for word processing and moral support. I also want to thank Katherine H. Hill for her dedicated copy editing and collegial conversation, and Randy Gadikian for countless cups of coffee and listening. And special thanks go to my family: James, Heather, and Alexander, who inspire and encourage me; my mom, Ruth Phelps, who did a good deal of child care; and Nancy Weekly, a valued friend and colleague.

Maryruth Phelps Glogowski
Editor

Chapter 1

INTRODUCTION

Maryruth Phelps Glogowski

Libraries are exciting places to work. New knowledge is assimilated every day into the collection in the form of books, journals, electronic files, audiovisuals, manuscripts, and software. The 1990s are presenting academic libraries with unprecedented technological demands and a restructuring of higher education that has drastically reduced personnel and materials budgets. Change is a constant. Training is one of the critical functions of a library that aspires to maintain quality. This volume has been compiled to help academic librarians provide the necessary training for library personnel.

Academic Libraries and Training presents chapters written by librarians and computer professionals from across North America, from Florida to Saskatchewan, from Texas to New York. There are many creative and practical ideas put forth. Technology played a role in producing this volume since many of the authors were selected after responding to a message posted on the Library Administration and Management mailing list. The use of the Internet can enrich library professional development immensely; so there is an article, "Electronic Discussion Groups: A Primer," that while not being a training article per se, does provide the necessary information for a librarian to take advantage of a new form of collegial exchange.

The experience and expertise shared in this volume is considerable. I am grateful to the authors for explicating their ideas. The articles are grouped into five broad areas: Staff Training and Orientation, Automation Training, Retraining, Staff Development, Networks and Electronic Access. Naturally, certain essays could fall into more than one area. Read broadly! There are many exciting and transferable projects detailed in these pages. I am sure the individual authors would welcome communication with colleagues wishing more detail.

August 15, 1992

STAFF TRAINING AND ORIENTATION

Chapter 2

THE *NEW HORIZONS IN LIBRARY TRAINING* PROGRAM:

COMPUTER-BASED TRAINING USING HYPERCARD

Pauline S. Bayne

INTRODUCTION

Funded by a research and demonstration grant from the U. S. Department of Education in 1989-90, a team of nine librarians from the University of Tennessee, Knoxville (UT) developed a series of *HyperCard*-based instructional units designed for staff training.[1] The program is called *New Horizons in Library Training: Computer-based Training for Library Staff*. It has been in use at UT for all newly-hired students and full-time support staff since January 1991 and has been distributed widely to other interested libraries. During the fifteen-month development period, Apple Computer, Inc. also supported the project with technical assistance and an equipment grant.

WHY COMPUTER-BASED TRAINING?

Employee training does occur in academic libraries, but it is rarely a systematic, basic introduction to the mechanisms of library work or the service mission of the library as a whole. Typically, training occurs within departments on a one-to-one and job-specific basis.

This mode of staff training is time-intensive, expensive, and usually too specific to deal with general library issues such as appropriate referral patterns, positive service attitudes, or preservation concerns. Job-specific training will always be necessary and is probably best designed and implemented at the unit level. Yet certainly it would be beneficial to introduce all new employees to the organization and teach them the basic skills and concepts of library operations. It would be more efficient to teach some basic library skills—such as the classification system used—in a centralized program that minimizes supervisory involvement but adds competency-based assessment. Supervisors could then create their training programs knowing that employees came to them with at least a common set of instruction.

Computer-based training (CBT) or computer-assisted instruction (CAI) is a proven educational method in use for many subjects and all levels of student abilities. Computer-assisted learning programs offer a number of advantages. They are interactive, allow the learner to control the pacing and sequence of instruction (see Figure 1), provide appropriate and timely feedback, and may decrease the amount of time required for the instruction. Multimedia learning materials address individual learning

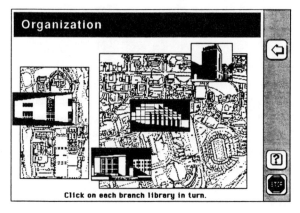

Figure 1.   Menus like this one permit trainees to view instructional sequences in the order they prefer. Sometimes they must view all portions; at other times, they view as much as they want or need.

preferences (aural, visual, and kinesthetic). Such programs can also keep accurate records automatically.[2]

Yet, CBT has not been used extensively for library staff training, probably because the market is not large enough to support commercial products, and not enough librarians have been willing to learn computer programming in order to create them. The cost of hiring programmers to develop specific library units has been prohibitive for libraries. However, by 1988, the combination of increasing numbers of microcomputers in libraries and a new inexpensive software program, *HyperCard*, provided an opportunity for librarians to create their own computer-based training program. At the University of Tennessee, a group of librarians set out to demonstrate the effectiveness and efficiencies of computer-based training as one component in a library staff training program.

WHY *HyperCard*?

HyperCard, a hypertext software program for the Macintosh, was developed by Bill Atkinson and released late in 1987.[3] It quickly fostered many applications in higher education. Instructional programs described in the Fall 1988 issue of *Wheels for the Mind* illustrated the widespread acceptance of this software and its use by people who had little or no training in programming.[4]

Because *HyperCard* programming (called scripting) rests in English-language phrases and is intuitive in formulation (see Figure 2), it allows the subject specialist (librarian), not programmer, to create specialized applications such as library CBT. *HyperCard* scripting permits the branching, drill, and testing of interactive CBT (see Figure 3); it also allows integration of sound, pictures, graphics, animation, and video that make a learning session interesting and call on all the senses used to transfer information.

Other similar programs, such as *SuperCard*[5] and *Course Builder*[6], were available during project planning, but the directors chose *HyperCard* for reasons of economy and ease of use. University of Tennessee developers intended to make the CBT

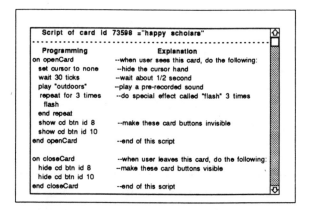

Figure 2. A sample of *HyperTalk* scripting (or programming).

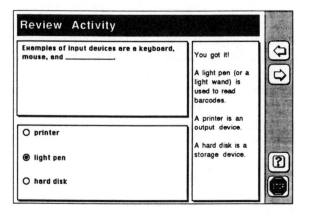

Figure 3. Learning is reinforced by review activities and by test questions for certain units. The answer panel on the right is shown as it would be after the trainee had chosen correctly.

units available to other libraries and allow modifications of the units to fit local circumstances. Therefore, the cost factor for other libraries was important, and *HyperCard* was the least expensive software of its type. In the late 1980s, purchase of a Macintosh computer included *HyperCard* software at no extra cost; the software cost $49 if purchased separately.[7] The availability of this computer hardware platform and inexpensive software was a primary reason for its use as the authoring language for the CBT demonstration project.

CBT DEVELOPMENT

Topic Selection

In September 1989, prior to the official start of the grant period (October 1989 - December 1990), project planners conducted a survey of training needs within the University of Tennessee, Knoxville Libraries. The Libraries, with a collection exceeding 1.7 million volumes, serve a student body of 26,000 with 48 faculty, 130 staff, and approximately 150 student assistants. Administrators, department heads, faculty, and selected supervisors ranked eleven potential topics, suggested others, and responded to attitudinal questions about the use of computer-based instruction. Respondents gave overwhelming approval for this approach to training: 100% indicated that CBT could be effective for some staff training, and 96% gave their support for a CBT program for all new staff. The response rate was almost 80%. This survey was the first step in staff participation, planned to improve "buy-in" to the library-wide training program.

Based on the internal needs assessment, the development team prepared a survey instrument to be sent to Association of Research Libraries' directors or personnel officers. The survey asked for priority ranking of nine possible staff training topics and explained that the materials would be made available to other libraries when completed. The response rate for this survey was 71%.

The team used both surveys to determine the list of six topics for development: orientation to libraries, access to periodicals, computers in libraries, acquisition and organization of collection materials, reference services, and resource sharing. Project directors had developed a prototype unit on Library of Congress classification prior to funding of the project; it was revised to match the screen design and instructional patterns chosen for the other training units.

Team Approach

The two project directors, Joe C. Rader and Pauline S. Bayne, chose the other seven team members because of their interest and ability but also to represent various library staff constituencies—public services, technical services, the personnel and automation departments, and branch libraries. Training opportunities arranged for the team included self-instruction books and online tutorials for *HyperCard* self-instruction, a two-day *HyperCard/HyperTalk* workshop, a half-day instructional design workshop, and a session on graphic design.

The team was organized into coauthor groups so that at least two people were responsible for development of each unit. Developers relied on a team approach throughout the development phase (April through October 1990), meeting monthly to share ideas and critique the work of coauthors. Considering everything from choice of fonts to glossary terms to specific instructional text resulted in "pre-tested" materials. Even before staff evaluators examined the units, at least seven individuals had had the opportunity to suggest improvements.

Coauthors began by conceptualizing the instruction to be provided, developing metaphors, and designing images to convey messages effectively. They created an initial script for each unit in a *HyperCard* "planning stack," which like a storyboard included instructional text along with ideas for production—such as animation or special effects—and graphic images or sounds that might be included to enhance the instruction. Team members received each planning stack, in print and as a *HyperCard* stack, for review. Group criticism aided coauthors to revise both concepts and presentation ideas before beginning production of the units.

In April, the team completed uniform screen designs including a variety of instructional screens; menu, glossary (see Figure 4), and help screens; and consistent navigational devices (see Figure 5).

Project directors relied on advice from the team as they developed various stacks and mechanisms needed to bring the separate training units together into a coherent program. These materials included "front end" stacks, providing a title sequence, help stack,

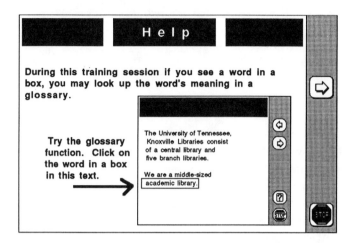

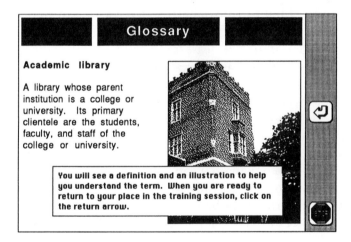

Figure 4. An illustrated glossary is available in the CBT units.
Trainees may click on any word bracketed by a box
to see a definition. They return to their place in the unit
by choosing the return arrow.

trainee registration mechanism, an onscreen evaluation form, and
the programming to gather use data and create data reports.

Figure 5. A consistent screen design helps trainees to navigate
through the units. The vertical bar on the right contains forward
and backward buttons, a help button, and a stop button.
The horizontal bar provides headings for topical sections
of the training unit.

Development Time

The federal grant provided 10% released time for seven team
members and 50% released time for two project directors for twelve
months. A no-cost extension of three months brought the project
period to 15 months, from October 1989 through December 1991.
Much more time than originally allocated was necessary to
complete the project, but it was difficult to track separately the time
involved for various aspects of the project: team training,
development, evaluation, and implementation planning. The
total time spent on the project was 4,788 hours. Development and
evaluation of the instructional materials probably took two-thirds
of that time (3,192 hours) while training, implementation
planning, and other administrative tasks accounted for the rest.

EVALUATION METHODS

Individual topical units were completed at various times from
August through October. As finished, each unit entered a three-

stage evaluation program in which library staff members experienced the training units and made comments. The first two evaluation stages were periods of formative evaluation, designed to gather information from evaluators leading to revision and improvement in the instructional material. Formative evaluation helps to identify mechanical problems, such as unclear explanations, missing information, typographical and grammatical errors, or test questions and explanations that are not correct. In the computer-based environment, techniques of formative evaluation are used to identify animation and graphics that do not operate correctly or do not enhance the instruction, dead ends in branching, mechanisms (such as glossary or navigation buttons) that do not operate, sequences that are too fast or too slow, and other problems related to information as communicated through sight and sound on the computer.

The first evaluation stage included both one-on-one evaluation and expert review. One-on-one evaluation allowed two or three employees to review each unit while being observed by one of the unit's coauthors. Expert review permitted all team members to critique each unit on a screen-by-screen basis using an interactive "comment button." Coauthors revised each unit based upon these initial evaluations.

For the second evaluation stage, the team selected a group of thirteen staff members, representing a variety of demographic factors, as evaluators. Each reviewer received instructions on computer use and reviewing procedures for the first unit. Then he or she proceeded through the other units independently, completed an.evaluation questionnaire for each, and answered a comparative questionnaire after the final session. Again coauthors revised instructional content and presentation methods after this evaluation round.

Evaluation stage three required a field test designed to evaluate the intended training environment—procedures to be followed and characteristics of the training facility. In this case, selected team members set up a training room and instructed 15 library supervisors in how to start new employees in the program. These supervisors then introduced 22 newly-hired staff and student employees, from 11 different departments, to CBT. Each new employee completed the prescribed units and a program evaluation. These supervisors also introduced other current staff members to the program bringing the total number of participants in the field test to 49.

CBT IMPLEMENTATION

Implementation Concepts

The project directors (Bayne and Rader) were joined by Personnel Librarian, Jillian Keally, to form an implementation planning group only one-third of the way into the project period. They identified three assumptions that guided development of implementation procedures:

1. Broad, general library training is work-related and beneficial for all new employees.
2. Responsibility for success of work-related training must rest with the employee's supervisor.
3. Involvement in development of materials or the training process will enhance acceptance of the program.

Belief in these assumptions led planners to offer a variety of presentation and discussion sessions to department heads and supervisors and to involve a large number of staff in evaluation activities. Rather than designate one order for training units within the program, they asked department heads to decide the best order of units for their new full-time employees; and, for student assistants, to choose which units as well as the order of presentation. The plan, as implemented at UT, requires that support staff take all seven training sessions within the first six months of employment, beginning with *Orientation* during their first two weeks on the job. Student assistants take from one to seven of the training units starting with *Orientation*.

Using checklists for each trainee and data collected within the CBT units, both supervisors and Library Personnel Office staff monitor the progress of trainees. Checklists provide a paper trail for scheduled sessions, guide trainees in the desired sequence of units, and serve as certification of completion when returned by supervisors to the Library Personnel Office. Programming within the *HyperCard* stacks collects data unobtrusively on all users of the system. The trainee registers by typing his/her name, department, and selecting the appropriate employee status. The program records this information in a data file along with session name, start and stop times, test scores, missed questions, and trainee comments. Personnel staff collect the machine-recorded data weekly and produce reports for their office and for supervisors. Cumulative data is then available for periodic assessment of the entire program.

Facilities and Equipment

Employees in the central library complete their training sessions in a small training room equipped with six Macintosh computers. This equipment is reserved for computer-based training and available only to library staff. On the UT campus, three buildings house the five branch libraries; therefore, project directors placed three computers in these locations. Here the priority use is computer-based training but other software is available, and staff may use the computers for other purposes. At each training location, trainees may reserve computer time for their sessions on a scheduling calendar.

CBT Procedures

When an employee is hired, the Library Personnel Office sends the appropriate CBT checklist to the individual's supervisor. Within two weeks, the supervisor schedules an introductory session for the new employee. In this session, the supervisor introduces the Macintosh computer using part one of the "Apple Tour of the Macintosh" or "Macintosh Basics"[8] to make sure the individual is comfortable in using a mouse to choose items on the computer screen. The supervisor also teaches the following procedures: (1) scheduling sessions and using the training room/ computer, (2) using the CBT checklist, (3) starting each session with the program menu and registration, (4) ending each session with the "Stop" button (which causes user data to be recorded and the computer to shut down), and (5) reporting problems. This introductory session takes about thirty minutes. From then on the trainee works independently to complete each unit as scheduled by the supervisor.

BEYOND UT

Generic Instruction

From the beginning, the project directors intended for these training units to be distributed to other libraries. Credits and acknowledgments on the title screen of each unit invite such use and provide distribution information. As far as possible, developers created "generic" instructional materials for use in many libraries. The one unit that is an exception is "Orientation," which serves as a model of CBT for orienting staff to the library.

Modification of Local Information

Trainees view local information—such as the names and locations of library departments or specific circulation or processing practices—by choosing buttons that display loops of cards or fields of information (see Figure 6). Modifications may be made by: (1) removing the local buttons, leaving their related cards in place but without access, or (2) replacing UT images and information. In replacing information, access to a scanner is important, as is familiarity with *HyperCard* operations. The quantity of local information is small, approximately 125 screens out of 1,760 in 6 training units, or 7% of the total.

How long does such modification take? The implementation group (Bayne, Keally, and Rader) took on a follow-up project to test various aspects of implementation at another institution. In the summer of 1991, working with Gail Kennedy and a team of librarians at the University of Kentucky (UK), they decided to replace the local information in all training units, to create a brief

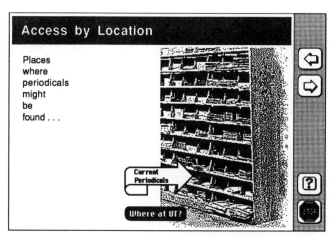

Access by Location

Places
where
periodicals
might
be
found . . .

Current
Periodicals

Where at UT?

Figure 6. The "Where at UT" button leads the trainee to maps and information specific to this institution. This button may be removed or the screens it leads to may be replaced to modify the training unit for use in another library.

UK-specific orientation unit based on part of the UT model, to convert the stacks from *HyperCard* 1.2 to *HyperCard* 2.0, and to administer pre-and post-tests to a group of new UK Library employees having no prior exposure to computer-based training in the library workplace. University of Kentucky implementation testing occurred between September 1991 and February 1992 in computer laboratories used both by university students and library staff.

For this use, the modification process required scanning photographs and drawings, removal and replacement of information, design of a new menu screen, and replacement of the "Stop" button programming to bring each trainee back to the program menu rather than to "Shutdown." Replacement of local information in six training units required about eighty hours. The stacks also had to be converted to *HyperCard* 2.0, the software version in use at the University of Kentucky. Such conversion occurs very quickly but then requires painstaking review of each CBT stack. Changing the version and checking took about fifteen hours.

Distribution

Bayne and Rader announced availability of the program in April 1991 by sending a printed brochure, *New Directions in Library Training,* to ARL libraries, electronic mail announcements to five electronic mailing/discussion lists for librarians nationwide, and press releases to library journals. Since then more than 230 requests for information have been filled, and 75 sets of diskettes have been ordered. A survey of those who have requested information or ordered the stacks is under way to learn how and where these staff training materials are used.

Developers arranged two distribution methods for the *HyperCard* stacks, either by purchase of diskettes or electronic transfer of the files. Libraries or individuals may order copies of the CBT stacks (14 diskettes, *HyperCard* version 1.2.x) at a cost of $25.00 from the Apple Library Template Exchange[9] or download the stacks electronically using standard File Transfer Protocol (FTP) on the Internet (Internet address: UTKLIB.LIB-.UTK.EDU or 128.169.201.210). Diskette copies and informational brochures deposited with the LOEX (Library Orientation Instruction Exchange) Clearinghouse,[10] may be borrowed for examination. Also, a program brochure, project report (also published as ERIC document ED 333 902) and FTP instructions are available from the project directors.[11]

Future Developments

Activities to build on the existing CBT program and expertise are already underway or in a planning stage at UT. Representative are a one-year review of the full implementation of the program with some revision of training units expected, development of additional units for the library-wide program (e.g., on preservation of materials), creation of complementary units for department-level training, expansion of units to multimedia, and adaptation of some parts of the instruction for user education.

CONCLUSION

The University of Tennessee, Knoxville Libraries' research and demonstration project has achieved its goal of innovative utilization of technology to meet a national library need for efficient and effective staff training materials. The project demonstrated that librarians, who are not computer programmers, can use *HyperCard* as an authoring tool for instructional units. The response of evaluators throughout the development and testing phases indicated that a machine-assisted method and the training materials themselves can be enjoyable and successful for library trainees. The implementation plan, developed and used for more than a year at UT, showed that such a program can be instituted on a library-wide basis.

Distribution of the CBT units to other libraries means that training materials, not available commercially, are now available to thousands of academic libraries. Furthermore, any library having at least one Macintosh computer and at least one interested librarian can quickly tailor six of the seven units to suit practices of its institution. Of course, it will take the involvement of many more librarians and staff to transfer the UT-developed training materials to an accepted and viable library-wide training program in another setting. Project developers look forward to responses of librarians external to the University of Tennessee as they review and use these materials.

NOTES

1. *Computer-based Training for Library Staff: A Demonstration Project Using HyperCard,* October 1, 1989-December 31, 1990. Grant number R 197-D900-40, funded by the College Library Technology and Cooperation Grant Program, Higher Education Act, Title II-D, CFDA No. 84.197, Research and Demonstration Projects. Pauline S. Bayne and Joe C. Rader were principal investigators; coauthors on the team included William Britten, Agnes Grady, Jillian Keally, Martha E. Rudolph, Steve R. Thomas, Alan Wallace, and Judy Webster.

2. Nathan M. Smith, "Designing Effective Computer-based Instruction Systems" in Mary Piette and Nathan M. Smith, *Project F.O.R.E.* (Logan, UT: Utah State University Library, April 1991), 6.

3. Hypertext is "a means of connecting information in a non-linear fashion with a computer automating the process for moving from one piece of information to another." (S. Jong, "The Challenge of Hypertext," in *Proceedings, 35th ITCC* [Washington, DC: Society for Technical Communication, 1988], 30).

4.   *Wheels for the Mind* (Cupertino, CA: Apple Computer, Inc.) 4 (Fall 1988).

5.   *Aldus SuperCard 1.6,* available from Silicon Beach Software, Inc., in 1992 was priced at $299.

6.   *CourseBuilder Version 4* is available from TeleRobotics International, Inc., Knoxville, TN in 1992 at a cost of $995.

7.   Today, run-time versions of *HyperCard* 2.x are distributed with new computers by Apple Computer, Inc.; developer's versions were available in 1992 for purchase from Claris Corp., priced at $199.

8.   These tutorial materials come on diskette with a Macintosh computer. The first part of each introduces use of the mouse.

9.   Apple Library Template Exchange, Apple Library Users Group, 19381 Bandley Drive, M.S. 8-C, Cupertino, CA 95014.

10.   LOEX, Library, Eastern Michigan University, Ypsilanti, MI 48197.

11.   Project directors Pauline S. Bayne and Joe C. Rader may be reached by mail at The University of Tennessee, Knoxville Libraries, 1000 Volunteer Blvd., Knoxville, TN 37996-1000 or through electronic mail:
BITNET: BAYNE@UTKVX, RADER@UTKVX;
INTERNET: BAYNE@UTKVX.UTK.EDU, RADER@UTKVX.UTK.EDU.

SUPPLEMENTAL BIBLIOGRAPHY

Graphic Design

Metros, Susan E. "Process + Product: An Equation for Computer Enhanced Creative Problem Solving." *Proceedings: National Computer Graphics Association* (1990): 409-25.

HyperCard Stacks

Apple Library Users Group. *Apple Library Template Exchange Catalog.* Cupertino, CA: Apple Computer, Inc., 1992.

ALUG: Apple Library Users Group Newsletter. Cupertino, CA: Apple Computer, Inc.

Instructional Design

Dick, Walter and Lou Carey. *The Systematic Design of Instruction,* 2d edition. Glenview, IL: Scott, Foresman and Company, 1985.

Tessmer, Martin, David Jonassen, and David C. Caverly. *A Nonprogrammer's Guide to Designing Instruction for Microcomputers.* Englewood, CO: Libraries Unlimited, 1989.

Chapter 3

A TRAINEE'S PERSPECTIVE

Tessa Killian

INTRODUCTION

My first quarter at Antioch College is about to come to a close. I relocated myself to southwest Ohio to begin a position as serials librarian. I would like to share my experiences as a "new hire" in the hope that my story might benefit both students of library science about to go on the job market and seasoned librarians given the task of understanding the mind-set of the entry level librarian. Obviously everyone's experiences will be different, and libraries of varying sizes and types will place different demands on their employees, but perhaps new librarians reading my testimony will be better equipped to confront the training experience that lies ahead.

I was hired at Antioch to succeed their retiring serials librarian. Some background on the college would be helpful in understanding and interpreting my experience. Antioch is a small but growing liberal arts college located in southwest Ohio. It was founded in 1852 by Antioch's first president, Horace Mann, and the current cooperative education program was adopted in the 1920s by Arthur Morgan. The college operates on a quarter system. Students spend six to seven quarters during their college career working either paid or voluntary co-op jobs, learning as much as possible about diverse work environments. Students could be working with Navajo Indians in New Mexico, or for a corporation in a large metropolitan area. In order to graduate in four years the students carry large course loads during the quarters spent on campus. Rather than receiving grades for their classes, students receive evaluations from their professors. Antioch offers a truly distinctive liberal arts education, which prepares students for the world of work through cooperative work programs and study.

My co-workers are the most dedicated group of people I have ever worked with, and the demands on them are plenty. They have to be dedicated to run a library this size with a small staff while maintaining an unyielding emphasis on providing the best service for the Antioch community. Four librarians and four support-staff operate the library, which is open ninety-one hours per week during the last half of the academic quarter. The library houses about 300,000 volumes, including bound periodicals and subscribes to over 1,000 periodicals, a large collection for a student body of 734 students. The library also runs the college microcomputer center and houses the college archives.

I was hired as a serials librarian responsible for current periodicals and standing orders. As the serials librarian at such a small college, however, I am also responsible for reference duties, as are all of the other librarians, and scheduled to work evenings and alternating weekends. Actually, reference work is a large part of my daily routine. I am asked reference questions periodically throughout the day because the serials office is located next to the reference section and the CD-ROM indexes. My duties also include occasional bibliographic instruction.

TRAINING

I received on-the-job training, which began my first day of work. For the first week I was trained by the retiring librarian, then by the head librarian, my direct supervisor. Training was done on an ad hoc basis as opposed to systematically. According to a statement from a 1990 NASIG workshop report, "The kind of in-house training undertaken by libraries varies according to the size and scope of the collection, the types of materials acquired and retained, and the status and role of the serials librarian."[1] All of these factors, as well as the number of library employees and the library budget, played a role in determining the nature of the on-the-job training I received.

Still, my first day of work at my first full-time library job was the most frustrating day of my life. I went home and called my loved ones, running up major phone bills, trying to talk through my anxieties. During my first day, I learned how to sort the mail and check in the periodicals—seemingly simple tasks. Yet, this was not taught in library school. In fact, what I knew about serials I had learned in a chapter from my collection development text book and as a student worker in the library. As a student, I had previously worked in an acquisitions department with an online system, so I never realized how much was involved when this process was done manually. In fact, there is not a single computer in the serials office. I use an old IBM typewriter with carbon paper to write my correspondence and claim letters. This is more a sign of the fiscal times than a reflection of anachronistic methods. Trade-offs have to be made between spending on collection development and computerization, and Antioch clearly prefers to maintain the integrity of their periodicals collection.

The workloads of the other librarians left them little time to train me. This restriction was reflected in the nature of the training process. Furthermore, the sheer amount of work that needed to be done in the library required that I hit the ground running. They needed me there to work and there was little opportunity for long introductions, orientations, or extended tours of the library's collection. For example, on my first day I was also shown how to close the library building—another seemingly simple task. There are about four pages of detailed steps to complete this procedure, right down to every latch, light switch, and door lock. Prior to the start of the academic quarter I closed the building for a whole month and, on occasion, forgot some steps.

After the retiring librarian left, I was on my own with the few pages of notes that she left me. The head librarian had at one time been the serials librarian and is personally responsible for developing the excellent periodicals collection which the library houses today. He thus took over my training. With his guidance, I learned how to perform several of the duties I would be responsible for, such as claiming missing or damaged periodicals and processing invoices. I had several questions every day that I would ask my supervisor, who was more than willing to help because he wanted to ensure that I was performing the tasks efficiently.

For a while, I was very confused as to exactly what my duties as serials librarian were. I had no job description, and, thus had some unclear expectations about my job duties. For example, I am a serials librarian in a library with very few employees, and as such, spend much of my time doing clerical work, unlike professionals in larger, better equipped libraries with clerical staff. And the head librarian and circulation supervisor handle all of the periodical binding duties. I have learned that everybody in such a small library, librarians and support staff, must wear several hats. In my case: serials librarian, serials clerk, bibliographic instruction librarian, and reference librarian.

Like serials training, reference training takes time and is very library-specific. My supervisor would occasionally show me an excellent source, which I was not familiar with, but I had no formal training to familiarize me with this specific reference collection. It has taken much time to apply my reference training from school and previous work experience to the collection at this library, to perform as a quality professional reference librarian. Each library has a different scope to its collection, but has some key sources. But where are they? I cannot yet walk to them with my eyes closed. I have to find out where that book lies on the shelf. Sometimes the book I want isn't there. Where is it? We do not have it, but have some equivalent source I do not yet know about. For example, I could not find *Facts On File*, which I had used frequently at other libraries, but I found out that instead we have *Keesing's Record of World Events*. This occurred on several occasions. Also, I found that some items may be classified differently. For example, I could not locate the *Encyclopedia of Associations*. At the library where I had previously worked, this source was given a call number starting with AY. At Antioch, it was given a call number starting with H. Another library trainee has called this "new place disorientation."[2] This happens when the source of the reference answer is known, but for various reasons it cannot be located on the shelf. For months, I would find myself thinking of a book I wanted to use to answer a question, forgetting the title, and my mind would go to the shelf of the library where I had previously worked. Then I would picture the call number or title and try to find it here at Antioch. After four months, I still do this on occasion. This problem can be solved only by becoming familiar with the library's collection over time. It is necessary, but by no means easy, to integrate what was learned in reference courses with the current working situation.

A really positive aspect of my training was that I started working well before the beginning of the academic quarter, and since there was no summer school, the library was not very busy. As such, I could concentrate on learning my job. I spent a lot of time wandering through the reference stacks looking at titles. At the moment, I felt like I was wasting time, but I was really doing the right thing to become familiar with the reference collection. A full time library job is a wake-up of sorts after the gradual and controlled pace of library school. There is not time to browse anymore. When answering a reference question for class, I could take as long as I wanted to answer a question and look at the books around the key source. Now I have to deal with students who will wander off if I do not produce the answer to their question within a few minutes!

CONCLUSION

I was alone on duty my first Saturday afternoon on the job. I had to take care of the microcomputer room and circulation, as well as answering reference questions and closing the library. I was thankful that there were not many people around yet, because the important little things, like checking out books, were still new to me.

Now I get asked quick questions, for which the responses are never quick, while walking from one office to another. For example, a student asked me to help her find a photograph of a certain Belgian renaissance tapestry that she had recently seen. Just a few months ago this question would have really thrown me, not knowing what art books we have in reference, or where the Library of Congress Subject Headings were to find books in the stacks which would help to answer the question, but now I can cope.

I constantly feel like I am bothering my co-workers with

questions. But new things come up every day, things with which I have not yet had to deal, which I may or may not have been told about five months ago. Because I was so nervous the first few days of work, anything that was explained to me was lost forever. According to Sheila Creth this is not uncommon. She states that:

> During the initial period in a new job, the individual operates to a large extent in a vacuum regarding behavior and performance expectations, and lacks the full range of knowledge and skills needed to perform effectively. This situation generates some degree of nervousness and anxiety and will contribute to learning difficulties if the supervisor makes no attempt to minimize this legitimate anxiety.[3]

Some things happen over time, others have to be made to happen. I feel most confident performing the tasks where training was most emphasized. I needed to be shown how to perform certain tasks which are institution- specific, while mastering other aspects of my job were simply "a matter of time."

NOTES

1. Linda Meiseles, recorder, "The Do's and Don't's of Serials Training," [A report of a workshop at the 1991 NASIG Conference] *The Serials Librarian* 19, nos.3-4: 217-219 (1991).

2. Lois Walker, "All I Really Needed to Know I Didn't Learn in Library School," *North Carolina Libraries* 48: 259 (Winter 1991).

3. Sheila D. Creth, *Effective On-the-Job Training: Developing Library Human Resources* (Chicago: American Library Association, 1986), pp. 17-18.

Chapter 4

USE OF A CHECKLIST IN STAFF ORIENTATION:

A RESPONSE TO "A TRAINEE'S PERSPECTIVE"

Carol J. Richards

In "A Trainee's Perspective" Tessa Killian vividly describes her experiences as a new hire at Antioch College. The very heavy workload that Antioch's small staff is expected to carry and the incredible number of tasks that she, as an entry-level librarian, was expected to learn prompted her to describe her first day on the job as the most frustrating day of her life. Ms. Killian, it should be noted, received her training during the first week of her tenure from the retiring librarian she was replacing. Later, her immediate supervisor was her trainer.

Ms. Killian's introduction to her new position was probably not unlike that of many other new hires. She was fortunate to have had even a one-week overlap with the retiring librarian who could give her some insights into the position. Her comments about how frustrated she was are not surprising. Her colleagues' work load limited the time they could devote to orienting her to a very complex librarian position.

In most academic libraries the norm is to be short-staffed. Everyone usually has more to do than he or she has time to do it in. Unlike Tessa Killian's situation, in many libraries the employee who previously held the job, has left before the new employee arrives, and seldom is anyone assigned the sole task of training the new librarian. Efforts may be made to split up the task—the secretary will cover this, the office mate will cover that, and the department head will cover the other—with the hope that the new person will pick up all necessary information with time. In general this works. The new librarian learns, asks questions, is corrected. However, amazing gaps can inadvertently occur because no one thought to tell the new employee about something, and the new employee has to overcome enormous amounts of anxiety and frustration during those first few weeks on the job.

At E. H. Butler Library, Buffalo State College (State University of New York), the Information Services Department decided to try to alleviate some of the "new job stress" that is common to new employees. To systematize the introduction of new employees to the department an orientation checklist was developed in 1984. The checklist was designed to insure that the new hire would learn about the library and its operations in a reasonable amount of time.

The Butler Library staff has about 45 librarians and clerks serving a primarily undergraduate student population of some 13,000 students. The Information Services Department has a total of sixteen staff plus varying numbers of student assistants. The ten Information Services librarians work irregular schedules, which include night and weekend duty at the reference desk. As college faculty members they are also required to participate in scholarly and governance activities. In addition, they do materials selection, act as liaisons to academic departments, teach in the library instruction program, and perform online searches.

It is standard procedure for new employees at BSC to receive an appointment letter from the college instructing him or her to report to the library director's office on the first day of the job. The director's secretary takes care of any in-library red tape and then directs the new person to the college personnel department to take care of necessary paperwork. The employee returns to the library and goes to the department head's office to begin orientation.

The first day the department head or designee always reserves time to spend with the new employee, going through items 1 and 2 on the checklist, perhaps visiting certain locations and making introductions. No effort is made to go beyond items 1 and 2 to avoid overloading the new hire with information. The checklist itself is explained and given to the employee. The department head emphasizes that, from that point, it becomes the employee's responsibility to get through the rest of the items on the checklist, generally within two months. The time frame is deliberately long to avoid overwhelming the new employee, who has to concentrate on learning his or her daily responsibilities. The order in which the items are checked off is not important either. It is expected that there will be steady progress through all the items, allowing a person to proceed at a reasonable rate.

The primary duty of any new Information Services librarian is to work at the reference desk, so some time is set aside on the first day for the new person to "sit in" and observe during a two-hour shift at the reference desk. After that, a schedule of time to be at the desk with experienced reference librarians is prepared so that the new hire will know when he or she is "on the desk," and plans for other orientation activities for succeeding days are made. Also, the department head usually arranges to have several staff members go to lunch with the new person that first day. Furthermore, the new hire is directed to introduce himself or herself to anyone he or she encounters but has not yet met. He or she is also instructed to learn the reference collection, to learn his or her way around the rather large and complex building, and to observe reference transactions at every opportunity. With the reference desk schedule, the checklist, and the need to learn reference operations, the new hire can plan his or her time for "self-orientation." The checklist serves to insure that the new hire gets around to everyone and to every place..

Each librarian is hired to do a specific task, such as administering interlibrary loan, microforms, or audiovisual services. Training may be provided by the clerk who manages day to day operations in the area, by the department head, or by someone else. But general orientation to the milieu in which the new person will be working is an ongoing process that contributes to the individual's ability to perform well at the reference desk. It takes time. Giving each new employee the responsibility for his or her own orientation allows the individual to proceed at his or her own pace without feeling rushed or abandoned. The use of the checklist serves as a guide to the new hire, reassuring him or her that everything is being covered.

The checklist itself is under constant revision. It must be updated to reflect changes in personnel, in locations of resources, and in services offered. The department head generally reviews it each time someone is hired to insure that it will accurately guide the new person. It is specific about the Information Services Department. It also names the person that the new hire is expected to contact with regard to orientation to specific operations.

The cheerful cooperation of other staff is important to the success of the checklist approach. Library staff members are always advised that a new person is on board. They expect to meet with the new hire and plan to spend time explaining their operations. They are reminded what it is like to be the "new kid" and to make every effort to answer questions and to give thoughtful explanations of operations.

Where possible, documentation is given to the new hire. In addition to the checklist, the individual receives a packet of materials which usually includes the college view book, a campus map, a campus telephone directory, the latest faculty newsletter, the library staff directory, all library handouts and guides prepared for the public, copies of standard library forms, the procedures manual, and any other printed items that might be useful to a new hire.

The department head is the contact person for many items on the checklist, so the new hire meets often with the supervisor while working through the checklist. Feedback from the new hire is sought. Is something causing confusion? Is there doubt about some particular phase of library operations? The new hire is encouraged to ask questions of appropriate staff members. The fundamental reason for using the checklist is that the more one knows about library operations, the better he or she can perform the job.

In general, new Information Services librarians seem to become comfortable in their new positions reasonably quickly. They also learn to be tireless in asking questions about operations. The department head realizes that it might be prudent to review certain items at intervals, e.g., the complex personnel practices used by the library and the college and covered in item 7 of the checklist.

The use of a checklist has proven to be a convenient and reasonably efficient method of providing an introduction to Butler Library for new Information Services librarians. Its use can systematize the varied activities with which new personnel must become familiar. It also serves to assure that the new hire is learning what needs to be learned.

ORIENTATION CHECKLIST FOR LIBRARIANS

Information Services
E. H. Butler Library
Buffalo State University

This checklist is given to Information Services Librarians beginning employment with Butler Library to insure that they become familiar with all aspects of library resources, services, and procedures. It is expected that the librarian will go over the individual items on the checklist as time permits making sure he or she understands each one. In addition, it is expected that the librarian will take any available time to learn the reference collection and to practice using the available resources. All Information Services personnel welcome questions and will be delighted to "explain things."

1. General Butler Library information—Department Head

    — Job responsibilities
    — Supervisor's expectations
    — Hours
    — Meals and breaks
    — Lavatories
    — Attendance
    — Offfice space
    — Library keys
    — Entrances and exits
    — Telephones
    — Security issues

— Electronic security systems
— Equipment
— Supplies
— Computer access
— Photocopy services
— Clerical assistance
— Student assistants
— Problem patrons
— Disaster preparedness
— Building maintenance
— Coffee club
— Smoking

2. Meet the members of the department; learn where their offices are and what duties they perform:

[This section list the names, ranks or titles, office numbers, telephone numbers, and primary responsibilities of the sixteen other members of the department. Student Assistants are omitted from the checklist because they come and go so rapidly, but introductions are made as appropriate.]

3. Reference Service—Department Head

— Philosophy
— Desk procedures
— Keys
— Telephone procedures
— Calendars and schedules
— Opening and closing
— Classrooms and room schedules
— Supplies
— Equipment
— Heaters
— Shelving and shelf-reading procedures
— Index Tables
— Index Shelves
— Atlas Case
— Map Case

— Dictionary stands
— Reference Storage
— Basement Storage
— Telephone Books
— Term Paper Guides
— New Reference Books
— Chemical Abstracts
— British Parliamentary Papers
— Research Guides and Bibliographies
— Library handouts and floor plans
— SHERLOCK and collection locations
— Periodical holdings and locations
— CD-ROM sources
— Trouble-shooting reference equipment

4. Make appointment with the person in charge to learn about other library services:

[Specific people are named after each of the following.]

— Archives and Special Collections
— Circulation and Reserve
— Collection Development
— Creative Studies
— Curriculum Lab
— Database Searching
— Faculty/Staff Photocopy Service
— Interlibrary Loan
— Learning Systems
— Library Instruction
— Media Booking
— Microforms
— Special Services

5. Spend some time exploring the building:

— Quadrants and stairwells
— Classrooms

— Meeting rooms
— Roof Garden
— Computer Terminal Room
— Store Rooms
— Basement and Maintenance Balcony

6. You will also want to learn about:

[Specific people are named after each of the following.]

— Materials selection
— Academic Department Liaison program
— Library governance and committees
— United University Professions [faculty labor union]
— Department and faculty meetings
— Department and library communications systems

7. Personnel policies and evaluation procedures for:

— Term contract reappointments
— Promotion
— Continuing appointment
— Discretionary salary increase

Chapter 5

TRAINING VOLUNTEERS

Linda Marie Golian and Linda Lou Wiler

INTRODUCTION

The incessant demands of rapidly changing technologies and automation continuously challenge today's library employees. Eager library professionals and staff members are constantly retraining to maintain efficient and effective library services. The result is a perpetually shifting work force that creates voids in library staffing that volunteer workers can uniquely fill.

Diversified library tasks create volunteer opportunities for people of all ages and backgrounds. Libraries have developed specific programs for unemployed teenagers needing summer activities, beginning library professionals requiring internships, or retired seniors desiring to feel useful in their community.

In this automated age, library volunteers can assist with more than reshelving materials, slipping returned books, or date stamping magazines. The key to enabling library volunteers to provide sophisticated technological assistance lies with the library's ability to organize, recruit, screen, train, supervise, motivate, and appraise successfully these very special workers.

BACKGROUND

Historically, the United States has always been a nation of volunteers. From frontier barn raising to present-day volunteer leagues, over one quarter of the adult population has freely given of their time and energy. In 1974 nearly 37 million Americans engaged in some type of volunteer activity. Today these figures have almost tripled, with more than 98 million Americans volunteering in 1989.

Higher education and academic libraries are now enthusiastically espousing the many benefits of volunteer programs. Significant budget cuts, personnel freezes, and escalating periodical costs of the late 1980s were perhaps the necessary catalysts for the utilization of this highly effective library resource.

Previously, unfounded fears of the library staff prevented some academic libraries from developing useful volunteer programs. While there is some basis for concern, overall library staff apprehension is unsubstantiated. Volunteers do not take away library jobs, hurt material or personnel funding, avoid tedious everyday tasks for more exciting and desirable public activities, lack commitment, cause supervisory and management problems, act disloyally, or lack technological abilities.

Instead, a volunteer program provides libraries many opportunities to use their resources, collections, and staff in more efficient and unique applications. The program participants enhance the library's operations by assisting regular library staff in day to day business, giving a fresh work perspective and contributing expertise not readily available. Volunteers permit the creative library to do more with less, initiate new ideas, save money, and experiment with new programs. Volunteers allow a depersonalized computer environment to become warm and human, and bring a different dimension to the academic experience.

ORGANIZATION

The first step in developing a library volunteer program is educating the library staff and administration. A variety of materials and colorful presentations highlighting the volunteer's value to the busy organization will help lessen staff fears. For proper support of a volunteer program, it is crucial to develop staff commitment and understanding.

Educated administrators understand the true costs of proficient volunteers. Volunteers, like donated books, are not free. Rather, they are a wise investment that benefits any library system. Astute administrators make available fiscal and time commitments for a volunteer coordinator, program publicity, increased telephone calls, postage, computer time, training time, stationery and other overhead expenses. Without this support the library volunteer program will fail.

The most critical element to a successful volunteer program is the assigning/hiring of a competent volunteer coordinator. This influential person is responsible for the organization and smooth operation of the entire program. The volunteer coordinator's duties include:

1. Writing radio and television recruitment spots
2. Writing volunteer worker job descriptions
3. Planning motivational strategies for library staff and volunteer workers
4. Planning and implementing volunteer training sessions
5. Planning and implementing training session for volunteer supervisors
6. Fostering a library-wide air of cooperation and good will
7. Recruiting, interviewing, assessing, and placing volunteers
8. Coordinating and keeping *all* volunteer records
9. Providing feedback and work assessments to volunteers and library supervisors
10. Acting as an ombudsman between volunteers and library supervisors
11. Fine tuning program as needed.

Tips on Volunteer Record Keeping

1. One person should be in charge of maintaining all records and blank forms.
2. Suggested forms to have on hand include:
   a. Copies of written job descriptions
   b. Blank application forms
   c. Blank evaluation/appraisal forms
   d. Blank exit interview forms.

3. A file should be created for each volunteer. This file should include:
    a. Completed application form
    b. Up-to-date job description
    c. Special information card (contains such information as birthday, hire date, emergency contact, current address and phone, critical health information)
    d. Current work schedule
    e. Completed evaluations/appraisals
    f. Completed exit evaluation.

No matter how small the volunteer program, the coordinator should allow ample time for proper management, give special attention to planning and task assignments, and involve the entire library staff in identifying appropriate tasks for volunteers. With the library administrator's cooperation, the volunteer coordinator can determine the necessary task frequency, task priority level, and the necessary task skills. These preliminary procedures require organizational skills, clerical assistance, office supplies, computer access, and file cabinet space for productive management.   The final planning step involves creating detailed job descriptions that include specific information concerning required hours, volunteer title and necessary skills. The volunteer coordinator should maintain these and all other records on a computer database management system, taking full advantage of the computer's flexibility to update frequently changing information.

Essential Elements of a Volunteer Job Description

1. Volunteer's title (e.g., looseleaf filer, reference aide)
2. Supervisor's name and title
3. Necessary time commitment (e.g., six hours a week divided into two three-hour shifts)
4. Specific work schedule
5. Duties (Important: Be as specific as possible.)
6. Qualifications (e.g., as a looseleaf filer, volunteers need to have good eye and hand coordination, and the ability to read fine print)

7. Library provided training (e.g., library will provide ten hours of looseleaf filing training)
8. Evaluation criteria (e.g., supervisor conducts a semiannual review, based upon filing accuracy, binder conditions and filing expedience)
9. Brief statement of the importance of this job for the library

Recruitment

After completing preliminary activities such as writing job descriptions and assigning priorities to volunteer tasks, the program coordinator proceeds to the next crucial phase, recruitment. Finding the right person for a specific job is an art, requiring time, commitment and support from library administration. When properly managed, the recruitment phase insures a smooth-functioning volunteer program; inappropriately managed it is a catalyst to disaster.

Prepared Library Materials for Volunteer Recruitment

1. Posters
2. Flyers
3. Library brochures
4. Letter written by the volunteer coordinator or the library director briefly explaining program
5. Volunteer application forms

Recruitment is one method of educating the surrounding community about the library. Therefore, the program coordinator should conduct searches in a professional and courteous manner.

Over-recruitment is a common mistake made in many volunteer programs. A competent volunteer program coordinator begins with a small core of knowledgeable volunteers, and later builds upon this strong foundation. One suggestion for recruiting talented volunteers is to start with familiar people, like the members of library staff families.

Recruiting Sources for Library Volunteers

1. Vocational/technical centers and other computer training schools (a good way to get computer and word processing volunteers)
2. Library foundation/friends' membership rosters
3. Local area volunteer leagues
4. Local area churches and synagogues
5. Local area high schools
6. University student government and service clubs
7. Local retirement centers (a good source for midday clerical office volunteers)
8. Local chapters of national associations such as AARP, AAUW, NOW
9. Local library schools
10. Advertising on local radio, cable and television stations
11. Advertising in newspapers (local and school)
12. Memos to library staffs' families (spouses, children, parents, neighbors, etc.)
13. Posters placed in local businesses like grocery stores

Worthwhile recruitment is not a one-time effort. It is an endless activity that needs to be done regularly to provide the changing library with an infusion of enthusiastic recruits. These individuals will bring new skills, fresh ideas, and renewed zeal to the library volunteer program.

SCREENING

A well-managed recruitment campaign provides the library with an abundance of volunteer workers. Successful placement of these applicants requires a complete screening process.

To assure effective placement and training, cooperation between the various library supervisors and the volunteer coordinator is essential. This cooperation provides the inquiring program coordinator with a thorough knowledge of volunteer job opportunities and the necessary required skills.

Materials to Facilitate Screening Process

1. Application forms
2. Lists of possible interviewing questions which meet EEOC and affirmative action guidelines.
3. Comment/evaluation form (used by program coordinator after conducting interview)
4. Insurance/waiver forms
5. Personnel/emergency contact card

The Volunteer Job Application Form is an essential fact-finding and screening tool for the program coordinator to use. When thoughtfully constructed, this basic form provides crucial information not readily available from other screening sources. This form should be brief and simple, with ample space provided for detailed written responses. Open-ended questions should appear towards the end of the application form.

Essential Elements of a Volunteer Job Application Form

1. Name
2. Local address and telephone number
3. Permanent address and telephone number (necessary for volunteers who are part-time residents in your community)
4. Person to contact in case of emergency
5. Date of application
6. Beginning date
7. Method by which the volunteer gained knowledge about the program
8. Times available to work
9. Skills/background (this section can be a list of skills that applicants circle, such as word processing, typing)
10. Several open-ended questions such as:
    I work best when...
    I prefer jobs that involve...
11. References (contact a minimum of one reference for each volunteer applicant)

The program coordinator schedules personal interviews after reviewing applications. Interviews flourish in a relaxed and positive environment. Questions highlighting technological skills and experiences assist in accurately matching the volunteer to library tasks. Applicants need ample time to respond to this sensitive probing and to elaborate on their background.

During the interview the program coordinator maintains an enthusiastic attitude, and provides the applicant with a brief overview of the library's operation. This overview lessens volunteers' misconceptions concerning how they will fit into the overall library organization. The volunteer coordinator and other library supervisors involved with volunteers, should follow the same EEOC and affirmative action regulations that apply to the paid library staff when interviewing volunteer applicants.

Sample Questions for Interviewing Library Volunteers

1. Why are you interested in this volunteer job?
2. What do you hope to accomplish?
3. What are a few of your hobbies and interests?
4. Can you make a six month to one year time commitment?
5. Do you have a reliable means of transportation?
6. What do you already know about this library?
7. What would you like to know about this library?
8. Describe your computer experiences.

After applicant interviewing, the intricate process of matching volunteer skills and library requirements begins. An effective pairing process considers not only the skills and background of the volunteer, but the volunteer's personality, likes, dislikes, flexibility, and available hours. The coordinator carefully matches this information to the wants, needs, time restrictions, and supervisor's personality of the individual library departments. If a volunteer applicant does not fit into the library's overall workforce, the program coordinator should diplomatically thank the volunteer for applying, and tell the applicant that the library will keep the application on file. The program coordinator should not feel obligated to place every volunteer.

Suggested List of Activities for Volunteers

1. Help check out library materials.
2. Shelve library materials.
3. Read assigned shelves.
4. Help in taking library inventory.
5. Assist in bar coding collection.
6. Type bibliographies.
7. File looseleaf services.
8. Update CD-ROM journal listings.
9. Assist patrons using CD-ROM indexes.
10. Repair books.
11. Check in library materials.
12. Help patrons use microform and other audio-visual equipment.
13. Help with manual or automated record keeping such as overdue notices and serial claiming.

ASSIGNMENT

The program coordinator matches a volunteer's aptitudes with library openings, and then provides an opportunity for the volunteer to meet the prospective supervisor. Together, the volunteer and supervisor decide job responsibilities, specific work hours and other task-related expectations.

Both the supervisor and volunteer should discuss and sign an informal written contract. Elements such as volunteer job title, supervisor to whom the volunteer reports, time commitment, schedule, evaluation criteria, general duties, and the overall importance of the job to the library are an integral part of this agreement.

Job satisfaction is the result of properly matching program needs and the volunteer's desire for service. Clear job assignments and an understanding of procedures assist the program coordinator in this process.

ORIENTATION

The volunteer coordinator begins the volunteer's first day with a library orientation session, including information concerning office attire, protocol, and rules. Written handouts, library maps, guides, and library name tag (if used) help the volunteer easily understand the new environment. The coordinator addresses procedures such as time logs, injury while volunteering and grievance policies, concluding the orientation session with a complete library tour. During this tour, the program coordinator introduces the volunteer to other library co-workers.

TRAINING

All successful training programs involve trust, creativity, consistency and an overall element of caring. Therefore, effective volunteer programs should provide the same guidance, encouragement, support, and correction as accountable library employee training programs.

Training may be provided in a variety of ways, ranging from one-on-one instruction to small group presentations. However, individualized training, although time-consuming, is the most effective way to build improved task comprehension and a volunteer's self-esteem. One-on-one and hands-on-training is especially important for tasks involving automated systems, computers, audio-visual equipment, and the physical processing of books.

The supervisor should assess the volunteer's current skills and specific task knowledge before beginning an individualized training program. Consideration of the volunteer's learning style and preferences insure effective learning. When possible, the training program should accommodate these preferences.

The supervisor conducts training in a series of progressive steps, with each step reviewing previously learned materials. Teaching materials that stimulate a wide variety of learning senses, such as visual, auditory, and feeling, aid in the training process. As a final step, the trainer provides opportunities for review, practice, and remedial sessions.

Incorporation of available modern technology into the training process allows volunteers to practice in computer training files and tutorial programs. This is especially important for volunteers unaccustomed to working with personal computers.

The library environment is constantly changing, with advances in the technological domain occurring too rapidly for any one person to comprehend. It has become crucial for libraries to provide frequent training and retraining sessions for all library staff members, including volunteers. *Flexibility* is the most important key in any training program.

SUPERVISION

During the training process the library volunteer learns the assigned job and asks question when necessary. The supervisor explains tasks in a friendly and supportive atmosphere. This includes reviewing policies, procedures, and special rules before allowing the volunteer to work independently. These sessions should emphasize situations requiring referral to the supervisor.

The supervisor formulates assignments so they are easy to understand. Division of assignments into sections allows for their completion within the volunteer's assigned work schedule. Since many volunteers work short time spans, time management is a useful addition to the traditional training program.

Before the volunteer's arrival, the supervisor prepares work assignments by organizing the specific tasks. The necessary materials and back-up projects should await the volunteer for easy movement from one task to the next.

Supervisors need periodically to review assignments with the volunteer. Together they discuss current procedures and make any appropriate changes.

As in training, flexibility is significant for successful program supervision. A productive volunteer program also benefits from supportive, understanding, and patient supervisors.

MOTIVATION

Motivation is a critical element in any volunteer program. A supervisor pays volunteers with words and acknowledgment of accomplishments, not money. Volunteers need to know they are important and that their job assignments fulfill a needed role for the library.

An easy way to motivate volunteers is to make sure the job assignments match their skills, backgrounds, and current time limits. This allows volunteers to feel useful and successful in their library-related duties.

Little deeds mean a lot to a hard-working library volunteer. One reason people volunteer is the desire to do good while belonging to a group. Supervisors foster this feeling by assigning volunteers specific work spaces whenever possible. Privately assigned desks or individual mail trays give a sense of worth. Ample space for personal items such as sweaters, purses, and coffee mugs is the minimum of requirements.

Most staff members have some sort of work-related title (e.g., binding clerk). Giving library volunteers equivalent titles fosters a team spirit. For example, a volunteer helping a binding clerk process newly bound books might be a "binding volunteer."

Effective volunteer programs provide opportunities to recognize volunteer contributions on a regular and timely basis. They motivate volunteer workers by giving credit where and when credit is due, and by remembering to say "thank you."

Suggested Rewards and Motivators

1. Invite volunteers to participate in all library social functions.
2. Create a library volunteer of the month or year award.
3. Introduce volunteers and their activities in staff newsletter.
4. Give volunteers special appreciation gifts to use in library (e.g., coffee/tea/water cup).
5. Create a volunteers' plaque listing all volunteers and the years they worked.
6. Have special events for entire staff that honor and recognize volunteers (i.e., annual awards/appreciation party).
7. Give special recognition to long term volunteer service (i.e., five-year appreciation pins).

APPRAISAL

A work review or appraisal functions as an additional method of providing motivation and appreciation for volunteer workers. Like paid library workers, regularly scheduled appraisals are important for volunteers. A periodic appraisal allows the supervisor and the volunteer to review the highlights and the troubled areas of a volunteer's past performance.

There should be no surprises in an appraisal. A good supervisor keeps the volunteer constantly informed concerning work performance throughout the appraisal period. Frequent informal meetings, with the supervisor asking volunteers for their comments and opinions concerning their library performance and task assignments, accomplish this purpose.

Both the program coordinator and immediate supervisor should frequently provide volunteers the opportunity to appraise and give feedback about the volunteer program. A vested interest in the library's welfare, expressed in pride of task accomplishment, is achievable when supervisors and volunteers form open and honest lines of communication.

During the appraisal interview, the supervisor should ask specific questions about the volunteer's experience and the volunteer program. "Did the library provide you with adequate training? Can you offer any suggestions to improve the program? What do you like best about the volunteer program? Do you wish to continue volunteering? Would you like to rotate to another area of the library?"

The library staff should also be given the opportunity to review the volunteer program and provide feedback. Staff members contribute additional insights for program improvements, and alert the volunteer program coordinator to changing library volunteer staffing demands and additional training needs.

A successful volunteer program requires constant improvement and program refinement. Changes are the natural result of an effective system.

Common Mistakes Made While Developing Volunteer Programs

1. Limiting gifted volunteer workers to trivial tasks

2. Assigning capable volunteers unsuitable jobs for their backgrounds and talents
3. Starving volunteers for feedback
4. Forgetting to say "thank you"
5. Neglecting to create a special area for volunteers to put their personal belongings such as, a purse

DEPARTURE

There are times when program changes, or transferring the volunteer to another library unit, cannot help or correct problems associated with a specific volunteer worker. Supervisors and program coordinators typically feel reluctant to dismiss volunteers not meeting basic program standards. However, time spent on a problem volunteer reduces resources needed for running an efficient volunteer program.

Dismissal should be the last resort for volunteers with problems such as, absenteeism, compulsive talking, inability to perform specific tasks, or accuracy difficulties. Program coordinators need to investigate thoroughly why a volunteer is experiencing a specific problem. Did the library provide adequate training and supervision? Did the volunteer understand the job assignment? Does the volunteer have some type of handicap, such as a hearing loss, that is causing the problem?

Sometimes, additional volunteer training or job assignment review results in a change to the appropriate and desired work behavior. When this does not occur, the program coordinator may need to firmly, but tactfully, discuss the troublesome performance with the volunteer.

Program coordinators need to view persistent problems in a special light. When internal solutions fail, the coordinator should suggest diplomatically that the problem volunteer might assist some other establishment.

To assist in the dismissal process, the supervisor documents *all* instances of inappropriate volunteer behavior. This documentation is necessary for the library's defense in the rare legal situation. The same information also allows the program coordinator quickly to spot specific behavior problems and patterns, allowing for proactive, instead of reactive, program planning.

All library volunteers, including dismissed workers, act as public relations agents. Therefore, the program coordinator, library administrators, and staff members need to treat the dismissed volunteer with respect and dignity. "Thank yous" to the volunteer for assistance given allow the volunteer an opportunity to leave with a positive feeling.

Highly skilled volunteers will end their employment for a variety of reasons, as do paid employees. Some examples include moving, finding permanent employment, or family conflicts. An additional responsibility of the program coordinator is to insure that skilled library volunteers do not leave due to administrative or personnel conflicts. The good coordinator explores why a volunteer is leaving during the exit interview, analyzes this information, and then corrects any perceived program problems as quickly as possible.

A successful program requires that all volunteers complete each step, including application, scheduled reviews, training, retraining, and the exit interview. These actions aid the continual growth of an effective and efficient volunteer library program for both the library and the volunteers.

LEGAL CONSIDERATIONS

The volunteer coordinator includes legal considerations in every step of the volunteer program. Common sense will usually provide good guidance, but when questions arise a consultation with the university/college attorney is appropriate. Minimally, the program coordinator and library director should inform the institution's personnel department and attorney's office before the formal establishment of a volunteer program.

Compounding the need for a legal consultation is the current mass of state, federal, and local laws governing volunteers. Every library's jurisdiction is unique and will have specific regulations and restraints governing its operations. Legal advice on insurance, waivers, and recommended record keeping is essential.

Most library volunteer programs do not contract trouble because of gross negligence upon the part of a volunteer or the library. Instead, most problems occur due to a minor misunderstanding, a planning deficiency or a lack of preventive measures.

An injured worker is a common volunteer program concern. The volunteer can hold the library legally responsible if injured while conducting a task within the scope of assigned library duties. Therefore, library administrators should have insurance policies inspected for volunteer coverage. If the insurance covers volunteers, policies should be further scrutinized to insure that provided protection is adequate. If the institution's insurance policy does not cover volunteers, a signed waiver form can release the library in case of injury. The college or university attorney should approve this form.

Legal Check List

1. Have a waiver written and approved by the university attorney.
2. Check university insurance coverage.
3. Become familiar with worker compensation laws.
4. Write disclaimers into waiver forms.

CONCLUSION

Rapidly changing technologies, perpetually shifting labor forces, and work flow modifications create voids in everyday library staffing that volunteer workers can fill. Under the guidance of a competent and enthusiastic program coordinator, a well planned and supported volunteer program will flourish.

Essential components of a volunteer program include: recruitment, screening, training, supervision, motivation, appraisal, and departure. The productive execution of these crucial parts creates a very special role for volunteer workers in today's technological library environment.

REFERENCES

Austin, Neville. "'But We Meant Well!' The Liability of Good Samaritans and Charities and Their Volunteers." *Philanthropist* 8 (Summer 1989): 3-15.

Bencit, Carol and Jensen, Ana E. *Performance Appraisal Development in a Volunteer Program.* San Francisco: Paper presented at the Annual Meeting of the Speech Communication Association, ERIC Document Number ED 315 829, (1989).

Biddle, William W. *Encouraging Community Development.* New York: Holt, Rinehart and Winston, (1968).

Castellucci, Arthur. *Volunteer Mother Program.* King of Prussia, PA: Research and Information Services for Education, ERIC Document Number ED 129 307, (1976).

Desautels, Diane C. "Discrimination Law—Statutory Protection for Volunteers Against Discrimination." *Western New England Law Review* 11 (Winter 1989): 93-142.

Dychtwald, Ken, and Flower, Joe. *Age Wave: The Challenges and Opportunities of an Aging America.* Los Angeles: Jeremy P. Tarcher, (1989).

Fletcher, Kathleen Brown. *Nine Keys to Successful Volunteer Programs.* Rockville, MD: Taft, (1987).

Hartmann, David W. "Volunteer Immunity: Maintaining the Vitality of the Third Sector of Our Economy." *University of Bridgeport Law Review* 10 (Winter 1989): 63-81.

Ilsley, Paul J. and Niemi, John A. *Recruiting and Training Volunteers.* New York: McGraw Hill, (1981).

Kim, Choongso. *The All-Volunteer Force: A 1979 Profile and Some Issues. Research on Youth Employment and Employability Development.* Youth Knowledge Development Report 2.8. Ohio State University, Columbus. Center for Human Resource Research, ERIC Document Number ED 203 059, (1980).

Kuras, Christine. *Volunteer Assistance in the Library.* California: Inglewood Public Library. ERIC Document Number ED 111 399, (1975).

Longfellow, Ellen A. "Volunteers and Liability." *Current Municipal Problems* 14 (Spring 1988): 447-451.

McCauley, Elfrieda. "Volunteers? Yes!" *School Library Journal* 22 (May 1976): 29-33.

McGrath, Marsha and Fine, Jana R. "Teen Volunteers in the Library." *Public Libraries* 29 (January/February 1990): 24-28.

McHenry, Cheryl A. "Library Volunteers: Recruiting, Motivating, Keeping Them." *School Library Journal* 34 (May 1988): 44-47.

Moyer, Mel. "Riding the Third Wave: The Growing Need for Trained Volunteer Administrators." *Philanthropist* 9 (Winter 1990): 41-47.

Naylor, Harriet H. *Volunteers Today—Finding, Training and Working with Them.* New York: University Press, (1967).

Pearson, Henry G. "Interviewing Volunteer Applicants for Skills." *Voluntary Action Leadership* (Summer 1986): 15-18.

United States Federal Domestic Volunteer Agency. *VISTA Handbook for Volunteers and Sponsors.* Washington, DC: Government Printing Office (1988).

Library of Congress National Library Service for the Blind and Physically Handicapped. *Volunteers in Network Libraries: A Manual of Procedures.* Washington, DC: Government Printing Office, 1986. ERIC Document Number ED 279 322.

United States National Center for Service-learning. *Service Learning: A Guide for College Students.* Washington, DC: Government Printing Office, 1980.

AUTOMATION TRAINING

Chapter 6

USING PROFESSIONAL TRAINING TECHNIQUES FOR LIBRARY AUTOMATION PROJECTS

Joanna M. Walsh

Recent concern with American competitiveness in the international economy has encouraged studies such as the Bureau of Labor Statistics' *Education and Training of American Workers*[1] and the National Center on Education and the Economy's *America's Choice: High Skills or Low Wages!*[2] These and other studies have focused on the knowledge gap in the workplace and the need for new skills training, as well as more information on what training is currently performed. They have identified the importance of training to the ability of workers to perform competently.

Implementation of new automation in a library certainly qualifies as new skills training. This can be as simple as adding a new CD-ROM database or as complex as installing a major integrated system with multiple functions. Typically, a variety of automation projects can be ongoing at any one time. Management of the training of library staff for these is a complex task.

A survey conducted by the American Society for Training and Development in 1984 found that American businesses spent $30 billion directly on training in one year.[3] That training was most likely developed and presented by training professionals. These trainers typically use the processes of Needs Analysis, Training Planning, Scheduling, and Evaluation to manage training. This article focuses on how these elements can be applied effectively to library staff training for automation implementation with particular emphasis on the training plan.

The basic concept of training is to fill the gap between the tasks to be performed and the skill level of the performer. Thus, the first step is a needs analysis to determine the appropriate tasks to perform and the abilities of the assigned workers at the current performance standard. The work to be done and the educational and/or skill requirements of those doing them are identified most comprehensively by a needs analysis. Once that is accomplished, a training plan is created to address the gaps identified by the needs analysis. The training plan identifies and details necessary types of training that may range from traditional classroom instruction to availability of necessary documentation at the worker site. A schedule accompanies the training plan linking the training need with the most appropriate time to learn it. Finally, methods of evaluation are determined, both to evaluate the training itself and its impact on task performance. These steps of training are covered in detail below.

NEEDS ANALYSIS

The first objective of a needs analysis is to benchmark the present level of performance of library functions. Part of this is to identify who is performing tasks, to determine the skills and education required for them, to identify resources available in the organizational climate, and to review existing systems and procedures with an eye to working smarter. In a perfect world, this process is part of the development of functional requirements for the automated system. A library manager should know how various automated functions will impact performance and functional requirements identify what is needed to improve performance. A comparison of the benchmark of current performance to the requirements for the new functions will allow the establishment of objectives for new performance functions. Even if the library does not incorporate needs analysis into the process of system selection, it can conduct a more limited performance analysis to compare current skills to those required by the new automated functions.

There are many means for needs analysis. Survey research is an effective way to determine staff capabilities—both perceived and actual—with interviews, questionnaires, attitude surveys, or tests. A typical outcome of survey research is an audience profile used to determine types of necessary training. Task and system analysis can include flow charting, work distribution studies, and analyses of present versus proposed jobs. This assists in determining the content of training. Field observation is another method that introduces a disinterested observer. This can provide a different perspective, but may intimidate participants. A records check can review job descriptions, performance appraisals, documentation, statistics, error reports, and other records both for current task analysis and relevancy for new skills. Finally, simulation, such as case analysis or role playing can provide valuable information for new skills training.

Ideally, a library should perform a needs analysis. However, in reality, this may not occur because of the organizational climate. Management support may be limited due to a lack of understanding of the value of a needs analysis given the time spent on it. If the system has already been selected, it may be seen as a fait accompli without need of analysis. Staff support will vary based on the perception of how the new functions will impact them; there will be hostility and fear as well as enthusiasm. A needs analysis, however, is the most effective means of identifying and understanding all of the training requirements as needed by that library. A well-prepared needs analysis and training plan will help influence senior management on the importance of training.

TRAINING PLAN

The next step after the needs analysis is to prepare a training plan. This plan should include all of the training required, not just vendor training. The following five basic components should be covered for each type of training:

- Audience
- Content (including methods and tools)
- Length
- Sources
- Cost

Audience

A basic element of training is to define the audience for a particular type of training as specifically as possible. This can be determined by exercising the "need to know" rule of selection. Only those staff who must have this training to do their jobs should be included. In the case of automation training, many staff will need training in the same area but their "need to know" may vary significantly. This allows for segmentation of the types of training to best suit the audience. Line staff at the circulation desk who perform actual functions will receive different training than managers requiring overall, but not detailed, knowledge of the system. A segmented audience can be further defined by varying levels. Thus, work-study students at the desk may receive almost identical content training to full-time regular staff but the training method will vary according to specific educational and skill levels and learning styles. The audience profile prepared as part of the needs analysis is very useful in determining audience segmentation and levels. The task analysis portion of the needs analysis will aid in defining the "need to know;" that is, what functions must be performed.

Many staff experiencing automation implementations complain of lack of information. Communication is a critical factor in the success of an implementation. All library staff should be kept informed and up-to-date. This can reduce the fear of change considerably and make staff feel like participants in the process, rather than victims of it. This communication, however, is a part of change management, not training. Staff should not confuse "need to know" training with a failure on the part of management to communicate about the automation implementation. "Need to know" focuses on what is critical for optimal performance so that training can be very focused and available training time maximized.

As opposed to the education of children and youth, professional training acknowledges that its audience is adult learners who learn differently than high school or college students. Malcolm Knowles has done considerable research and writing in the area of adult learning,[4] including the following general observations:

- Adults are self-directing; therefore, they want to control their own learning.
- Adults learn better by experience.
- Adults want what they learn to have validity for their life— either in or outside their job.
- Adults want to apply what they learn immediately.
- Adults want immediate success from what they learn (e.g., improved performance).
- Adults see learning as building blocks; (i.e., one skill learned should be the basis for the next).

In addition, learning ability remains constant for adults, although the speed at which they learn and relearn may vary. Adults, however, expect to learn. And, as any presenter of continuing education knows, a comfortable physical environment in which to learn is critical for adults. In particular, the environment should accommodate the hearing and vision levels of all participants. And, since hearing begins to decline after age 14 and vision after the early 20s, this will include most participants.[5] These general principles must be applied to the content portion of a training plan in order for it to be a success.

Content

Content is derived from training objectives developed from the needs analysis. Many training departments have developers who either perform needs analysis or use pre-existing ones to determine course objectives. These developers then prepare the content for each type of training, focusing on the methods and tools used, as well as the actual content. Content presented in a training plan can range from a brief description to a detailed syllabus. It is important that the content is described in enough detail so that the next step of development is possible. For example, a content description for Reserve Book Room training should include objectives, outline of content, methods, and tools.

Objectives

- Trainees will be able to apply library policies.
- Trainees will successfully operate Reserve Book function.

Contents: Basic presentation of functions of Reserve Book Room including:

- Creation of course lists
- Interaction with faculty in setting up reserves
- Creation of reserve secondary collection and addition of non-library materials
- Checking in and out using various loan periods
- Articulating and managing reserve book policies to users
- Managing busy periods
- Keeping and interpreting statistics

Method and Tools

- Method used will be classroom instruction with two-member teams sharing a system terminal in the training lab.
- Tools are vendor documentation and a flipchart for later use. Handouts will include worksheets and instruction outlines.

Methods for instruction vary and have been impacted by increased awareness of how adults learn and by the advent of computer-based instruction. Classroom and instructor-led training are still the most commonplace. Role playing, problem-solving, and case studies are typical methods, and skill transfer and motivation are typical techniques by which this type of training uses a knowledge of how adults learn. Workplace-based and competency-based instruction are increasingly favored as applicable to the need of adults to apply what they learn to a real-life setting, to use learning as building blocks, and to learn at their own pace. Workplace-based instruction can include: using specific examples from that library; determining how library procedures and organization fit into the new system before the training and incorporating those into the new skills training; and training on the actual equipment to be used on the job. Competency-based instruction sets objectives for different competencies rather than a general objective for one training session. Baselines for each competency are derived from the needs analysis and used to determine content for each competency. Trainees then learn at their own speed, building one competency upon another.

Computer-based instruction also supports the concept that adults learn better in hands-on, one-on-one situations or in small groups—rather than a classroom—and is readily adaptable to competency-based training as well. Computer-based instruction (also called CBI or CBT) is currently "hot"—for good reasons. Inexpensive, readily accessible, personal computers are available for computer-based instruction. The training is very portable and inexpensive to repeat. The number of trainees at any one time can vary and there is a high degree of flexibility with regard to scheduled time. It also eliminates one of the most expensive aspects of training—instructor time. Many library system vendors, as well as other businesses, are using computer-based instruction. The above advantages are even greater when used with an automated product since users are instructed on the computer (or one very similar) that they will use for their work, thus promoting comfort and familiarity. Students typically spend less time with computer-based instruction than with instructors.

There are, however, disadvantages to computer-based instruction: it is not appropriate for all types of training; it is best suited for basic introductions; it is passive and cannot answer questions; and it cannot alter the presentation based on student needs or abilities. An instructor would have that flexibility.

Computer-based training is also very expensive to develop—about 400 percent more than non-computer-based training. Thus, it is very important that, when computer-based instruction is selected, it really is the most appropriate method. In addition, just as libraries need to add their own training to augment vendor-provided instructor-led training, so they must be careful to account for the loss of benefits of that type of training when computer-based training is used. Often recommended is an additional preliminary session with staff who are afraid or uncomfortable with computer technology.[6]

Technology now presents many new methods for training, such as the use of expert systems (software using artificial intelligence to define responses), or hypertext (nonlinear database). The use of expert systems, however, is limited as they are best suited to very specific content and audience and updating is costly. Hypertext, on the other hand, is an excellent training development tool and can work well with the adult learning process. It is important, however, to select a method based on its appropriateness to the content and other components of the training plan and not simply because it is new technology.[7]

Tools for instruction are also included in the content portion of the training plan for each type of training. Typical tools include:

- Forms and reports
- Documentation
- Organizational communications
- Training materials

Forms and reports are usually examples of those tools used in the course of work for which training is provided. Documentation includes both that provided by one or more vendors and that created by the library. Documentation is a very important tool for use during a training session and afterwards. Vendor documentation rarely is sufficient, as it does not include specific library policies or procedures. In addition, there can be problems with poor indexing, inadequate examples, confused organization (in which manual to look?), and untimely updating. Organizational communications can include strategic plans, newsletters, memos, and other information important to job performance. Training materials can include worksheets, examples, books, or other materials. At a minimum, training materials should support the instruction but they can act as follow-up to the training as well. If transparencies or screens are used as examples, there should be printouts of them.

In some cases, a training tool can be a type of training as it is the best means to achieve a certain training objective. For example, a library experiences a high degree of error on the part of staff performing patron data entry. The needs analysis reveals that vendor-provided documentation is intimidating (several large volumes) and does not list the library-designed patron record data entry form. Staff were trained by a vendor representative on the vendor's schedule, which was several months before data entry began. As a result, they do not remember how to complete the data entry properly. In this case, the most appropriate training method may be a tool—for example, a flipchart that sits at the terminal and provides step-by-step procedures for entering the patron record.

Length

The training plan should also indicate the amount of time required for each training type. This is critical for overall management of training and scheduling. In addition, length is an important aspect of the design of the training. It is coordinated with a learning objective, content, and teaching techniques. The type of audience and the methods used will also influence the length. Practical matters, such as availability of space and staff, will also impact on length. It is best, however, to determine the optimal length based on the training design before imposing outside restraints.

Source

The training plan also includes the sources for each type of training. The source is whomever/whatever is providing the training. It is important to identify the best source for training before assigning the task based on availability or cost. The preparer of the training plan needs to become aware of all the alternative

sources available for the training and the most appropriate person
to provide it. Some possible sources are:

- The vendor
- Library staff
- Other staff on campus
- Other librarians expert in the area of the training
- Consultants
- Training companies

Regardless of the source, all training is part of the training plan.

The vendor will seem the most obvious source for much
automation training. Vendors typically offer training on their
system for a fee, although free or reduced-cost training is sometimes
offered by the vendor during contract negotiations or as a
marketing tool. The library should take advantage of this training,
but be aware of exactly what is offered, incorporating what is
lacking into the overall training plan. It is a good idea to get
complete details on training from the vendor during the system
selection process. This includes information on the vendor's
instructors and their level of expertise. Stories abound of library
staff who knew more during training than the newly hired
instructor from the vendor. There is also an opportunity to team-
train with vendor and library staff providing appropriate
instruction in their respective areas of knowledge. In these cases,
the library staff uses the information of what is lacking from the
vendor to prepare additional training.

A fact of life of any type of automation implementation is that
considerable training effort becomes part of the job description of
appropriate library staff. Often library staff are the only trainers
who can provide instruction in library policies and procedures and
in the relationship of the new system to other automated or manual
functions in the library. Vendors typically "train the trainer"
leaving the task of training additional library staff to just a vendor-
trained few. Library management must exercise care in whom they
select to receive this vendor training. These individuals should
have a commitment to and interest in training, the ability to teach,
and some experience in instruction. Those who go beyond simply

presenting the vendor training to develop and present non-vendor training should be even more experienced and capable.

There are often staff or faculty on campus experienced in systems who may be the most appropriate sources for types of training such as introduction to microcomputers, network technology, or troubleshooting problems. Using these resources can allow hard-pressed library staff trainers to focus on training for which they are uniquely qualified. It is important, however, to identify specifically (just as with a vendor) what will be taught so that the library still has some control over its staff training. Other librarians with expertise in the training type can also be an excellent source. Listings of those with experience implementing the same system or procedure are often available from the vendor or professional organization. Again, however, be sure that the person has appropriate training ability and experience.

Consultants or freelance librarians can be additional good sources for training especially when the library does not have staff expertise or available time. These individuals are also often available for training development. Training companies have many of the same advantages as consultants or free-lancers in that the library can focus on other aspects of the automation implementation while highly experienced trainers provide the instruction and/or development. However, the disadvantages are: lack of knowledge of the library (which can add to costs); and the fact that this is the most costly source of training other than the vendor. Some training companies have off-site locations that are an advantage if the library lacks adequate space or equipment.

Cost

Once the other components of the training plan are in place, the cost of each training type is determined. It is best to do this last so that all of the alternatives are identified regardless of cost. Cost includes the following elements:

- Development
- Cost of instructor(s)
- Location

- Development of tools
- Purchase of tools
- Supplies

Development costs add significantly to the total cost of training with one day of instructor-led training equivalent to thirty days of development time.[8] Libraries need to take this into account in developing training from scratch or customizing vendor-provided or pre-packaged training. Instructor costs will vary widely based on market value of their expertise and source of instructors. Every instructor has a cost—even so-called "gratis" library staff. Costs for library staff can be figured by indicating replacement costs for other duties, the cost to "hire" them for training, or however the organization calculates contributed services. There is typically little flexibility with vendors in negotiating the cost of instructors; this is more possible with consultants, freelancers, and many training companies.

Location costs can also vary considerably. It should not be assumed that on-campus will be less expensive than off-site, as some colleges and universities impose an automatic percentage of overhead. Length of training can also influence food costs associated with the number of meals and breaks provided.

Development of tools is expensive with the average cost of a piece of documentation at close to $100 per page. Purchase of tools includes: printing or photocopying costs, software purchase and licensing, and purchase and maintenance of equipment. Supplies for which costs must be calculated include folders, notebooks, pens or pencils, and name tags. Other costs might include travel, telephone, or support staff. A complete budget should be created for each training type. For more information on options in budgeting see Gary Matkin's *Effective Budgeting in Continuing Education.*[9]

SCHEDULE

Once the training plan is complete, a schedule for all anticipated training should be set. The comprehensiveness of the training plan allows for the scheduling of all training relating to the automation implementation. The first task is to prioritize the different types of training based on their relationship to the implementation schedule. That is, if the public access catalog (PAC) is the first piece of the new system to be implemented, training for the PAC is scheduled first. General introductory training can be scheduled early in the process to "warm up" library staff, but functional training (e.g., circulation procedures) should be scheduled as close to the actual implementation as possible. Remember that vendors must schedule a limited number of instructors for many customers. Many vendors have subject-matter experts who also do training. This expertise is especially valuable for complex functionality such as acquisitions or serials, but you may need to schedule that individual farther in advance. The second task is to schedule multi-part training, follow-up sessions, and retraining appropriately. It is also important to determine the development time required for library-developed training and make certain that it will be available when needed.

EVALUATION

Evaluation is a critical stage in training. It assesses the appropriateness of the training plan in meeting the training need identified by the needs analysis. Evaluation can be both immediate and long-term, program-wide, or specific to one training type. There should be at least one form of evaluation identified for each training type in the training plan. Paul Erickson[10] writes that, in general, an evaluation of one training type should answer the following questions:

- Were the defined training objectives met?
- Did trainees retain the content?
- Of that content retention, was the most important material retained?
- Were the methods used appropriate for the content?
- Did attendees increase their level of knowledge?
- Did trainees improve their job performance as a result of the training?

- Do the above elements vary in their success, depending on the instructor?

The most common form of evaluation used in library continuing education is the evaluation form ranking speakers, content, and the physical environment. Trainers derisively call these "smile sheets" as they rarely provide adequate evaluative information. Pre-tests and post-tests, however, are often used as a short-term measurement of competencies gained or content retained. Long-term review should also be built into the training plan to assist in planning further training or re-training. Testing, case studies, interviews, and performance appraisals are examples of appropriate long-term evaluation techniques.

Just as the evaluation of a particular training type links it to the original training need, so evaluation of the entire training program returns to the needs analysis and forms the basis for the next training plan. A model for a training program evaluation, as described by Theodore Kowalski, contains nine elements:

- purpose
- participation
- design
- time
- resources
- data collection
- data analysis
- decisions
- comparison with training objectives[11]

In conclusion, using the professional training techniques of Needs Analysis, a Training Plan, Scheduling, and Evaluation will help ensure a comprehensive approach to training for library automation projects. These techniques will also aid in developing an on-going training program in the library. While effort is required to apply these techniques, the reward is an awareness of exactly what is required to fill the gap between current staff skills and those required to perform successfully in an automated library.

NOTES

In addition to the references cited, there are several excellent sources of on-going information about training such as:

- *Training and Development Journal*
- *CLENEexchange* published by CLENE (Continuing Library Education Network and Exchange Roundtable), an American Library Association roundtable that is an opportunity to share information and experiences with other library trainers.
- Northeastern University, Boston, MA, holds an annual conference in the spring on adult teaching trends.

1.   *Education and Training of American Workers* (Washington, DC: Bureau of Labor Statistics, 1990).

2.   *America's Choice: High Skills or Low Wages!* (Rochester, NY: National Center on Education and the Economy, 1990).

3.   "What We Do and Don't Know about Training in the Workplace," *Monthly Labor Review* 113(October, 1990): 37.

4.   Malcolm S. Knowles, *The Modern Practice of Adult Education: From Pedagogy to Andragogy* (New York: Cambridge, the Adult Education Company, 1980), 43-59.

5.   Jane C. Zahn, "Differences Between Adults and Youth Affecting Learning," *Adult Education Journal* 17(Winter, 1967): 22-33.

6.   Joe Wehr, "Instructor-Led or Computer-Based: What Will Work Best for You," *Training and Development Journal* 42(June, 1988): 18-19.

7.   Clay Carr, "Making the Human-Computer Marriage Work," *Training and Development Journal* 42(May, 1988): 65-67.

8.   Wehr, 19.

9.   Gary W. Matkin, *Effective Budgeting in Continuing Education* (San Francisco, CA: Jossey-Bass, Inc., 1985).

10.   Paul Erickson, "Evaluating Training Results," *Training and Development Journal* 44(January, 1990): 20-23.

11.   Theodore J. Kowalski, *The Organization and Planning of Adult Education.* (Albany, NY: State University of New York Press, 1988), 157.

Chapter 7

TRAINING LIBRARY STAFF FOR SYSTEM CHANGES

Margaret R. Wells

Now, here, you see, it takes all the running you can do, to keep in the same place. If you want to get somewhere else, you must run at least twice as fast as that![1]

The Red Queen in Lewis Carroll's *Through the Looking Glass* echoes the feelings of many staff in today's libraries, where the rapid pace of automation change demands constant adjustments to new technologies and systems. Online systems are now a fact of life in most libraries, with computers standing in the former location of card catalogs, and orders, serials check-in records, circulation status, and other information formerly stored in paper files now visible to library staff and users in an online catalog. Staff in this dynamic environment must quickly adapt to system changes, constantly learning new skills and leaving old ones behind.

Changes to an existing online library system may be initiated by the software or hardware vendor, the institution, or the library. Vendor-initiated changes include software enhancements to improve functionality or correct system problems. Changes in institutional mission or local hardware support could also cause system changes. Decisions by the library include enhancing an online catalog by adding new databases to the system or changing to a completely new and different system. Sybrowsky discusses positive and negative reasons for system changes, ranging from the move to a more sophisticated and powerful system to a complete system change as a result of dissatisfaction with the vendor or total failure of the existing system.[2]

System changes are often incorporated under different circumstances from the initial introduction of an automated library system, including a compressed implementation schedule or with limited documentation or training from the vendor. In addition, the nature of training in the library usually evolves after the initial introduction of an integrated system, with training responsibilities moving from a centralized to a departmental function. Finally, staff accustomed to an existing system may resent the change, feeling threatened by having to learn new skills and relinquish their mastery of the system. As Lipow notes, "change... requires time to unlearn and time to be incompetent."[3] A comprehensive, well-organized training program helps staff succeed in this rapidly changing environment by reducing the stress associated with system changes.[4] System changes present exciting challenges for staff training, including the chance to evaluate previous training and devise new training strategies. Many authors cite the need for staff training in the automated environment, noting that "a well-designed and executed staff training program can effectively smooth the transition" to a new system.[5]

The information in this chapter is drawn from the literature of staff training and the experiences of the State University of New York at Buffalo Libraries in adding five periodical index databases to BISON (Buffalo Information System ONline), the Libraries' integrated online library system based on NOTIS software.[6] The index databases are produced by the H.W. Wilson Company[7] and loaded each month on to the University's mainframe computer which runs the BISON system. Users are presented with an opening menu listing six database choices: the online catalog covering most of the materials in the ten University Libraries, or any one of the five periodical index databases.

Most BISON modules were phased in to staff throughout 1990, with the public introduction of the online catalog in September. The periodical index databases were added to BISON in January,

1991, appearing to staff three days before becoming operational for users. The experience of the Libraries in training staff to use the original system and, later, the periodical index databases, proved the need to learn from experience, know the staff, communicate, build training content on existing knowledge, offer a variety of training opportunities, provide follow-up opportunities, and evaluate and redesign training. These principles are applicable to any organization involved in adapting to or planning for system changes.

LEARN FROM EXPERIENCE

Training literature and local experience provide valuable insights for training design. Glogoff and Flynn describe the experiences of the University of Delaware Library in training staff to use an integrated online library system and emphasize the application of adult learning theory, the use of on-the-job training techniques, the selection of effective trainers, and the need for strong administrative support for training.[8] Freeman and Clement offer additional insights for training program design, including the need for careful timing, accurate documentation, and training follow-up,[9] while Fetch and Rankka offer planning considerations for introducing an online catalog to staff.[10]

Staff evaluations of the introduction of an integrated online library system provide valuable planning information when changing the system. Previous training methodologies as well as staff assessments of the pace and content of earlier training should be examined to determine staff perceptions of which strategies were effective. The choice to require all staff to attend training, as is often the case when a new system is introduced, should also be reexamined when a system change is planned.

At the University at Buffalo, all staff (including supervisors) attended two two-hour "BISON Basics" workshops when the system became operational. These sessions covered all aspects of the system, including vendor background, hardware information, database and record structure, and an overview of all public and technical services processes. This training provided the foundation for later job-specific training sessions and was selected because, for the first time, public and technical services functions were accessible and visible to all staff using the system. The sessions mixed staff from all library departments.

Evaluations of "BISON Basics" training and staff comments about training for the Libraries' existing circulation system offered numerous insights. First, although some staff appreciated the opportunity to gain an overview of the entire system and learn how their work fit into it, others preferred learning only the skills required for their specific job functions and found the overview confusing. Training strategies recommended by vendors and the literature—such as having two people share a terminal during training sessions—were not as successful as expected. Many individuals noted that they preferred being active during sessions, and could not focus when watching someone else do the work. The strategy of mixing staff from all departments for the introductory sessions proved very successful and created an environment which illustrated that all levels of staff were learning together. This collegial atmosphere increased the effectiveness of the sessions by helping people feel comfortable about asking questions.

Evaluations of in-house training also revealed the need for training examples drawn from the actual work environment, rather than a reliance on the vendor-supplied training file. Many staff reported experiencing a lower rate of retention because examples did not reflect their daily worklife. Finally, staff comments on the evaluations reinforced the need to assess the familiarity of staff with libraries and computers before beginning training and offer introductory workshops as needed. Many of these assertions are supported by Epple, Gardner, and Warwick in their 1992 article on "Staff Training and Automated Systems: 20 Tips for Success."[11]

KNOW THE STAFF

An accurate awareness of the skill levels, learning styles, and interests of staff is particularly important when introducing system changes. Glogoff and Flynn offer an excellent example of a formal needs assessment survey in their 1990 article on "Front-End Analysis."[12] The instrument requests input on all aspects of staff training, including staff assessments of previous training experiences. Informal needs assessment methods include discussions with individuals or groups, a staff suggestion box, or requesting input through a notice in the staff newsletter. All levels of staff should be polled, including individuals who did not attend training.

The compressed timeframe for introducing system changes also necessitates targeting staff who will experience the greatest initial impact as a result of the change. Although all staff should be kept informed as system changes progress, the first training efforts may need to be geared to staff who need to teach others—whether users or staff—to make effective use of the new system. Training should allow time for staff to learn and practice the new features and then develop new policies or procedures as needed.

System changes also offer the opportunity to involve more people in training. Although a core of in-house trainers often exists from the initial implementation, these people might wish to limit or relinquish their responsibilities, offering others the opportunity to become involved. Contact people in each department or library—who are willing to learn the system, teach it to others, answer questions from staff, and be available when the new system becomes operational—help ease the transition. Adding new individuals to the training group distributes expertise and encourages a greater sense of staff ownership of the system.

Staff reactions to the existing system are useful when selecting trainers. Chiang offers a valuable summary of individual responses to change when she characterizes "the innovator," who is "able to work independent of tradition, to synthesize, and to pair needs with resources creatively;" the "adapter" who "can work from another institution's model to synthesize a local version;" the "mainstream type" who is "able to learn a new skill or develop expertise once the systems have been established in the institution;" and, finally, "staff who will always be hesitant about developing new skills or expertise" and require "cookbook procedures."[13]

Creth's list of desirable qualities of trainers is also useful when recruiting and selecting people to assist with system changes:

1. Ability to teach knowledge and skill to another person
2. Enjoyment of interacting and sharing knowledge with others
3. Openness to new ideas and suggestions
4. Ability to assess performance
5. Possession of a positive and constructive attitude toward the work, the department, the library, the supervisor, and the co-workers. [14]

All training should be geared to making the best use of staff at all levels, taking advantage of individual differences and interests to develop a comprehensive program.

COMMUNICATE

Decision-making and communication patterns in the organization have a direct impact on staff reactions to system changes. Staff who are involved in the changes and informed of all aspects of the implementation have a more positive reaction to system changes than those who feel that the decision-making is concentrated in a select group. Bichteler cites "dissatisfaction and frustration with the planning and implementation of automated systems"[15] as a major cause of stress for staff, noting the need to create an implementation committee representing all levels of staff, particularly individuals "who are influential among clerical and paraprofessional staff and those who may be skeptical."[16]

Communicating with all staff through the implementation committee, department supervisors, and the library "grapevine" helps provide accurate, timely information to staff before rumors based on misinformation begin. If the initial implementation was perceived by staff as forced upon them, with limited staff input in decisions, introducing system changes provides the opportunity to develop different communication patterns.

A staff newsletter creates awareness of the implementation progress by providing information on anticipated system changes. The newsletter could focus only on the system or be a regular column in an existing staff newsletter and should be distributed to all staff. When the system is operational, news articles on innovative uses of the system by staff help educate others and recognize staff ingenuity. A file of past newsletters provides a valuable historical chronicle of the implementation. "BISON Express" (originally titled "Take NOTIS") was introduced to library staff at the University at Buffalo about one year before the system was operational. Articles focused on the progress of the system, including technical information, the system naming contest, dates each module became operational, training schedules, and other landmarks in BISON history. When the staff changed to electronic mail, "BISON Express" changed with it.

Informational sessions open to all staff help alleviate anxiety about system changes and, in the absence of a test system, provide an opportunity for demonstrations through the use of handouts, transparencies, or dialing into other institutions which have the system operational. Informational sessions educate staff about how the system will change and assure people that training is included in the plan. The sessions should be held as soon as a plan for change is announced and structured around comparing the new and existing systems. Sessions should be offered at a variety of times to accommodate staff schedules and, in a decentralized environment, in different locations. Printed materials summarizing the content of each session should be made widely available.

Additional methods of communicating with staff include incorporating system progress reports into departmental and committee meetings on a regular basis. Marketing brochures or newsletters from the vendor also provide valuable information for staff. Finally, circulating or posting the minutes of implementation committee meetings keeps staff informed of and involved in current system issues.

STRUCTURE TRAINING AROUND
EXISTING KNOWLEDGE

System changes are less intimidating when the presentation of new knowledge is related to existing knowledge. Comparisons between the new and existing systems—including detailed, written descriptions of new ways to accomplish present functions—help staff make connections and synthesize new knowledge into their existing skills. When changes are introduced, staff are usually adept at the mechanics of the system, such as the operation of function keys or system commands, and can therefore focus on search strategies, the structure of new databases, and other transferable concepts.

The literature of adult learning and instructional design offers many insights relevant to structuring training content for system changes. Zemke and Zemke highlight the major characteristics of adult learning in their article on "30 Things We Know for Sure about Adult Learning,"[17] and cite Cross' observations based on the work of Cattell:

> First, the presentation of new information should be meaningful, and it should include aids that help the learner organize it and relate it to previously stored information. Second, it should be presented at a pace that permits mastery. Third, presentation of one idea at a time and minimization of competing intellectual demands should aid comprehension. Finally, frequent summarization should facilitate retention and recall.[18]

The Nurnberg Funnel: Designing Minimalist Instruction for Practical Computer Skill[19] offers an additional perspective, detailing the development of a training program to teach learners a defined set of computer skills. The author's recommendations are based on direct observations of learners, creating a program structured around: (1) allowing learners to start immediately on meaningfully realistic tasks, (2) reducing the amount of reading and other passive activity in training, and (3) helping to make errors and error recovery less traumatic and pedagogically productive.[20] These principles are applicable to many aspects of computer training and remind training designers of the need to structure knowledge differently for adults.

OFFER A VARIETY OF TRAINING OPPORTUNITIES

When a system change is introduced, staff familiarity with the existing system varies widely. In addition, many staff have probably exhibited a preference for certain learning styles, such as self-paced learning or attending workshops. This situation, combined with the logistics of introducing changes with limited lead time, demands planning for and offering an assortment of training opportunities. The specific strategies selected will depend on the needs and skill levels of staff, the resources available for training, and the magnitude of the system change.

Informational and help screens on the system provide an immediate vehicle for staff training and are usually accessible as soon as the system is operational. When properly designed to reflect the local setting, these screens provide point-of-use instruction and news about system changes for staff and users. Staff who do not attend training sessions, or will not use the new system regularly, may rely on these screens as a learning tool.

Many staff prefer formal workshops to learn content and then practice in the new system in a setting removed from the distractions of the workplace. [21] Depending on the magnitude of the system change, voluntary workshops for larger groups than initial training classes could be offered to the target staff first and the other staff later. A combination of brief and longer workshops structured around active learning techniques helps focus staff attention on the concepts they need to adapt to system changes. Baldwin and Williams offer useful suggestions for presenting training using active learning techniques.[22] Practice exercises based on actual examples suggested by staff increase relevance and retention.

Voluntary 90-minute or three-hour workshops for University at Buffalo Libraries staff for the periodical index databases began by reviewing the online catalog commands, database structure, and screen displays. This information was then compared and contrasted with the periodical index databases. The content of each database was discussed and compared to print versions of each index, which were available in many libraries. Training exercises began with familiar searches performed in the online catalog and then moved to the periodical index databases, with comparisons of the search results and an emphasis on the unique features of the new portion of the system.

Locally produced system documentation should be created as soon as possible and distributed to all major service points and any staff who request it. As Freeman and Clement note:

> No matter how clear and complete the system documentation is, a local policies and procedures manual must still be developed and maintained at each location for supervisory personnel. This in-house manual should include a description of the library's current policies as enforced by the system's parameters, such as loan limits and patron types.[23]

The manual also provides a vehicle for self-paced learning and quick reference use, particularly for individuals who do not attend training or regularly use the system. Different paper colors, index tabs, and a detailed index encourage easy use of the manual.

Quick reference guides—one- or two-sided sheets listing major system commands—are easy to create and could be the only training strategy needed. These guides provide a source for answers to basic system questions and also serve as a reminder to staff of the main system features. Quick guides should give the steps for each process and then provide examples. Visual appeal through the use of different typefaces, highlighting, and graphics, and posting the guides at each staff workstation increase their utility. When different databases are introduced, a "cheat sheet" highlighting the content and unique features of each could be created.

Additional supporting documentation created locally or by the vendor should also be widely distributed. For periodical index databases, a list of the journals covered in each helps familiarize staff with the coverage and disciplines included in each database. The introduction of periodical index databases often presents a need for staff to become familiar with sources and disciplines outside their traditional areas of expertise, such as science and technology for the humanities librarian. Supporting documentation assists with the learning process.

Practice exercises supplied to staff for use as a group or individual learning tool should focus on real questions and illustrate how to answer them on the system. When used for self-paced, individual learning, each question should have a single answer and search process. After staff are comfortable with the new features or system, questions illustrating a variety of approaches to arrive at the same or similar answers are appropriate. These questions could provide the basis for discussions in staff meetings or training workshops, with exceptional approaches highlighted in the staff newsletter to recognize creativity.

PROVIDE FOLLOW-UP OPPORTUNITIES

As staff experience with an automated library system increases, so do the number of questions and discoveries about the system. In the automated library, ongoing training is required to maintain staff skills, introduce new staff to the system, and help staff adapt to system changes. Allowing time for training follow-up reinforces staff knowledge and helps staff synthesize new skills. Involving staff in planning follow-up training helps increase the retention and transfer of knowledge.

Regularly scheduled refresher workshops on a variety of topics help maintain staff knowledge of the system and provide the opportunity to teach new skills. Assigning learning partners also helps staff practice and maintain their skills on the system. Lipow suggests these and other strategies to ensure the transfer of training, including the need for agreement on the objectives of training and the use of regularly scheduled progress reports from trainees.[24]

Additional means of reinforcing staff knowledge include the distribution of documentation updates to all service points and staff. Individual action plans setting training goals should be developed jointly by the supervisor and trainee. Skills checklists help staff track their knowledge of the system, identifying areas of mastery and areas requiring further practice. Demonstrations of staff discoveries about the system should be a focus of staff meetings and provide training as well as recognition. A quiet practice area and regularly scheduled training appointments allow individuals the opportunity to explore the system on their own, away from the distractions of the work area.

EVALUATE AND REDESIGN TRAINING

As experience and the literature demonstrate, evaluation is an essential component of effective training, but is sometimes overlooked as staff and trainers begin working on other aspects of the system or become involved in other projects. Whether written or verbal, formal or informal, some type of evaluation should be conducted and recorded after any system is introduced or changed. Questions asking quick facts as well as detailed opinions elicit comments on training successes and failures. Staff also need to be informed of the results of evaluations and actions based on staff comments. Evaluations could be used to provide an immediate assessment of a training workshop, or collected after staff have had time to use the system to assess the long-term impact of training. The effective use of evaluations to design new training and adapt present training illustrates the importance of staff in the process.

CONCLUSION

Automation and its associated changes will undoubtedly continue to present daily challenges for staff in all types of libraries. Whether adapting to a slight software change or learning a completely new system, staff need training to help them adapt to and make the most of change. A comprehensive staff training program involves individuals in the change process and creates a confident staff able to cope with and help users adapt to a wide range of new technologies.

NOTES

1.   Lewis Carroll, *Alice's Adventures in Wonderland; Through the Looking-Glass; The Hunting of the Snark* (New York: The Modern Library, 1925), 191.

2.   Paul K. Sybrowsky, "Changing Systems, The Vendor's Perspective: A Panel Discussion," *Library Software Review* 10 (January/February 1991): 25-26.

3.   Anne Grodzins Lipow, "Why Training Doesn't Stick: Who is to Blame?" *Library Trends* 38(Summer 1989): 65.

4. Julie Bichteler, "Technostress in Libraries: Causes, Effects and Solutions," *The Electronic Library* 5(October 1987): 282-287.

5. Margie Epple, Judy Gardner and Robert T. Warwick, "Staff Training and Automated Systems: 20 Tips for Success," *Journal of Academic Librarianship* 18(May 1992): 87.

6. NOTIS software is copyright NOTIS Systems, Inc., Evanston, IL.

7. Copyright H. W. Wilson Company, Inc., New York, NY.

8. Stuart Glogoff and James P. Flynn, "Developing a Systematic In-house Training Program for Integrated Library Systems," *College & Research Libraries* 48(November 1987): 528-536.

9. Gretchen Freeman and Russell Clement, "Critical Issues in Library Automation Staff Training," *The Electronic Library* 7 (April 1989): 76-82.

10. Deborah Fetch and Kristine Rankka, "Staff Training for an Online Public Catalog: A Practical Approach," *Library Software Review* 10(January/February 1991): 3-9.

11. Epple and others, "Staff Training."

12. Stuart J. Glogoff and James P. Flynn, "Front-end Analysis: Aligning Library Planning, Resources and Commitment to ILS Staff Training," *Journal of Library Administration* 12(1990): 25-26.

13. Katherine Chiang, "Computer Files in the Library: Training Issues," in *Computer Files and the Research Library*, ed. by Constance C. Gould (Mountain View, CA: The Research Libraries Group, 1990), 34.

14. Sheila D. Creth, *Effective On-the-Job Training: Developing Library Human Resources* (Chicago and London: American Library Association, 1986), 42.

15. Bichteler, "Technostress," 287.

16. Bichteler, "Technostress," 283.

17. Ron Zemke and Susan Zemke, "30 Things We Know for Sure about Adult Learning," *Training* 18(June 1981): 45-52; *Training* 25 (July 1988): 57-61 (reprint).

18. Zemke and Zemke, "30 Things," 60.

19. John M. Carroll, *The Nurnberg Funnel: Designing Minimalist Instruction for Practical Computer Skill* (Cambridge, MA; London, England: The MIT Press, 1990).

20. Carroll, *Nurnberg Funnel*, 7.

21. Epple and others, "Staff Training," 89; Freeman and Clement, "Critical Issues," 77.

22. Jill Baldwin and Hank Williams, *Active Learning: A Trainer's Guide* (Oxford, England: Basil Blackwell, Ltd., 1988).

23. Freeman and Clement, "Critical Issues," 80.

24. Lipow, "Why Training Doesn't Stick," 71.

RETRAINING

Chapter 8

CROSSING THE GREAT DIVIDE:
RETRAINING PUBLIC SERVICE
LIBRARIANS FOR TECHNICAL SERVICES

Kristin Senecal

There has historically been a great division in libraries, a gulf separating public services from technical services, and public service librarians from technical service librarians. In the last twenty years forces operating from within and without the profession have caused many to rethink that structure and the rationale that drives it. Librarianship has experienced a transition from the boom years of the sixties and early seventies to an era of declining enrollments, Proposition 13, and a host of factors that impact library budgets in a decidedly negative way. At the same time a wave of automation has swept through the library world, shaking up and blurring the lines of demarcation that previously defined and separated the profession. In 1979, Michael Gorman proposed a new vision for the role of the professional librarian, and by implication a new structure for libraries:

> The librarian, not just the future but also of today, needs to comprehend the importance of reader service, the intricacies of library automation, **and the nature and structures of bibliographic control.** The librarian must also possess a keen and analytical appreciation of the materials libraries collect. In this way librarianship will regain its professional pride, and cease to suffer from splintering and factionalism, and will become much more effective in economic and other practical terms.[1]

Gorman's vision in 1979 is even more compelling now, with the addition of runaway inflation in serials prices and an economic recession to the negative budgetary factors noted earlier. Automation has gained a firmer hold, its tentacles reaching into every aspect of librarianship. The two pressures of automation and budgetary restraint have gradually created an impetus toward centralization and away from the traditional compartmentalization of library work, a shift that has profound implications considering the current work force and its training for the profession.

Other pressures besides automation and declining budgets are at work breaking down the traditional divisions in libraries between public and technical services. The library literature has seen an increase in the number of articles discussing the dearth of professional catalogers, and more attention is being paid to a phenomenon known as "burnout," particularly as experienced by reference librarians.[2] Related to these discussions are numerous articles discussing job satisfaction—or lack of it—among librarians and a concept known as "holistic librarianship."[3] The latter is something that small libraries have been familiar with for years, since they could not afford the luxury of complete specialization and still man the reference desk and order and process all the materials. Midsized and large libraries are coming to recognize the potential of holistic librarianship: the midsized libraries because they are faced with staff cuts that may push them toward adopting small library models. The large libraries, including some of the largest university libraries, are looking at holistic librarianship due to a recognition that hierarchical, highly compartmentalized organizational structures impede the flow of communication necessary for the organization to function efficiently. Sometimes the divisions are so rigidly adhered to that the staff within them experience alienation, both from staff in other divisions and from the overall goals of the organization. There is the hoary time-honored stereotype of individual cataloging and reference librarians or even entire departments refusing to speak directly to each other, communicating only through an intermediary, usually a frustrated administrator. It is, unfortunately, a situation that is all too common, and anyone unlucky enough to have worked in such an environment can attest to just how uncomfortable and counterproductive it can be. The patron's needs tend to get lost in the no-man's-land between the two warring factions.

Several authors writing more recently on library administration have echoed and expanded on Gorman's thesis. John Cohn argues that "libraries must eliminate communication barriers and reduce unproductive conflict that inhibits effective networking. This may mean having to make structural changes in the organization of the library."[4] Dana Rooks, writing on the topic of motivating library staff, feels that "managers have come to recognize that strict adherence to the formal organizational structure defined by specialization and division of labor is no longer effective in today's society and with today's employees. These traditional structures...fail to provide for human needs within organizations."[5] Hugh Atkinson argues that the historical division of labor in libraries between reference, circulation, cataloging and acquisitions actually impedes the goal of serving the library patron. "The need for information is not related to the step in the library process at which the information is being handled."[6] Allen Veaner, in his book *Academic Librarianship in a Transformational Age*, puts it even more bluntly: "Functionally specialized, fragmented structures are more than obsolete; they are hazardous to survival."[7]

While midsized and large libraries are not rushing to demolish the walls between public and technical services, several have come to recognize the need to make changes at some level. In a survey of Association of Research Libraries performed in 1984, some crossover between technical and public service functions was found in 44 percent of the 81 respondents. Fifteen of these involved public service librarians participating in cataloging.[8] Two libraries on campuses in the University of California system, those at Riverside and Berkeley, instituted cross-training or staff rotation programs in the early eighties. At the same time the libraries at Texas A & M and Emory University were trying similar innovations.[9] In its evaluation Emory reported that "...participants at the conclusion of each exchange period have been enthusiastic and results have exceeded the expectations for the program."[10] Four librarians at the University at Albany (SUNY) took part in a cross-training experiment in 1987. Their response was similar to that reported at Emory University:

> The professional benefits of this project can be described as both technical and environmental in nature. Technical benefits reinforce the participants' skills or knowledge and result in greater self-sufficiency, while environmental benefits stress the importance of cooperation among professionals within the organization…In times of scarce resources and rapid technological change, it is doubly important that management provide opportunities for employees from different units of an organization to work together to develop common goals and to develop a sense of identification with the institution as a whole.[11]

MOTIVATION FOR RETRAINING

As a result of the forces discussed above, it seems that an increasing number of libraries would be interested in cross-training their professional librarians, for either a temporary or permanent shift in their responsibilities. In the past it has been more common to find technical services librarians cross-trained to work in public services. However, as noted earlier, the concept of training public service librarians to work in technical services, particularly cataloging, seems to be equally valid. If the present shortfall of professional librarians trained chiefly as catalogers continues, it may become a necessity.

The forces that may motivate an institution to implement cross-training have already been examined, but the motivation for the individual to participate in such a program is of equal importance. There are several reasons why librarians, particularly middle managers, may have reservations about implementing and/or taking part in cross-training. It is probably alien to what they were taught in graduate school, and is a radical departure from their on-the-job experience. The specter of undergoing additional training at this stage in their career may be daunting. A final, fundamental reason why professional librarians, particularly middle managers may resist cross-training lies in the perception that the potential or actual changes in their job descriptions as a result of cross-training will lessen their power and authority. Assuming the temporary status of trainee is relinquishing power to the trainer, however short-term the process. Cross-training is often accompanied by an organizational change, and the combination of these new experiences can be very threatening. People inherently resist change, especially if it is viewed as something over which they have no influence. To assuage these fears, the administration must do everything in its power to include the professional staff in decisions regarding cross-training and any accompanying reorganization.

Several strategies can be utilized to sell the library staff on the concept of cross-training. All of the staff affected by the proposed program must be offered an opportunity for input. In a large library situation, breaking down into small discussion groups to explore the ramifications of the change will allow for input and do much to allay resistance. A pilot program of cross-training staffed by volunteers could lead the way. After the training has taken place, the participants' reports of the experience and on-the-job performance may go further in convincing other staff than anything else. Indeed, experiments in cross-training may be generated by the rank-and-file, as was the case at the University at Albany (SUNY) mentioned earlier. The benefits of cross-training to the professional librarian in terms of job enhancement may be the most influential selling point when it comes to convincing staff to participate. The administration needs to keep up cross-training until a critical mass of employees have attained the desired competencies. A critical mass will have been achieved when those who possess the new skills set the dominant standard.[12]

When retraining public service librarians to work in cataloging, another stumbling block may be "cataloging anxiety." This malady can be described as the reluctance of a self-perceived "people person" to tackle learning what seems at first glance to be a maze of rules, regulations, and abstruse details and nit-picking under the domination of computers.

> To the general mystique of an arcane and abstruse codebook (AACR1 and 2) [is] added the extra fillip of computerization. The everyday language of MARC format [is] just another secret code to be cracked by the reference librarian. Today a cataloger no longer talks in card catalogese…but in a

cabalistic language of numbers—100 fields, 245 tags, filing factors, fixed fields, the 008. Catalogers learned the language of automation first...[13]

Catalogers may have learned it first, but the public services sector is now as deeply enmeshed in automation with its dependence on database searching and CD-ROMS. Indeed, with the arrival of EPIC and Firstsearch, the OCLC bibliographic database—and to an extent its cabalistic language—has become a familiar tool in many reference departments. Public service librarians may be surprised to find that the major tools of cataloging are much more familiar than they suppose.

The other assumption tied to cataloging anxiety is the suspicion that it is predictable work, with no intellectual challenge. Such assumptions are often based on how cataloging was taught in graduate school, or on practices from the past, before computerization liberated the cataloging professional from clerical duties. The appearance of OPACs and the national bibliographic utilities made it possible to shift the routine tasks of cataloging to support staff and radically changed the job descriptions of professional catalogers, a change that is often imperfectly understood by public services librarians. In fact, "the repetitious nature of cataloging activities has always been a myth and will remain so, at least until publishers and producers eschew any creativity in the presentation of bibliographic data and authors and artists eschew any creativity in their works."[14] Cataloging is an intellectual activity that requires constant decision-making that is anything but cut and dried. A certain amount of detective work also goes with the job, and knowledge of reference tools is definitely an aid in this aspect. In fact, Sheila Intner includes the latter as one of ten reasons why reference librarians would make good catalogers.[15]

IMPLEMENTING A PROGRAM

Once the decision is made to retrain librarians from public service departments for work in technical services, the policy-makers need to give adequate time and resources to the process, if it is to have any chance to succeed. Kathleen Bales describes the sequence needed in implementing any training program as following five steps: needs analysis, design, development, delivery, and evaluation. Needs analysis involves discovering the existing level of skills in the individual(s) being trained. Methods for ascertaining this information can include interviews, questionnaires, work samples, tests and guessing. Bales notes dryly that "guessing is probably the most widely used methodology in libraries."[16]

The design stage includes deciding how tasks can best be learned, and discovering whether qualified trainers are available within the institution. The initial response of most administrators would be to utilize in-house personnel as trainers. They have the knowledge of local practices and collections peculiar to the institution, and would probably be more cognizant of the institution's needs than an outside trainer. More than in-depth knowledge of cataloging and institutional procedures is needed; however, employees selected as trainers must have a willingness, even an eagerness, to teach others, and have demonstrated in their on-the-job relationships an above-average level of tact and patience. It can be a difficult transition to become the educator of one's professional peers or even superiors, hard to accept by both the trainer and the trainee(s).

Using in-house trainers has its drawbacks: it can be very expensive because of the loss of productivity in their normal assignments, especially in the initial design and development phases. Substantial release time will need to be allocated to allow for this time-consuming process. It is important that in-house trainers receive adequate time to devote to training planning and implementation, and recognition for these activities. The best solution for implementing a retraining program may lie in utilizing a mix of both in-house and outside trainers, with the latter concentrating on the needs analysis, design, and evaluation phases, and the in-house trainers providing the staffing for the development and delivery phases.

When in the design phase of a retraining program, it is of crucial importance to recognize the needs of adult learners. Adult learners require a high proportion of experiential learning, or learning by doing, in the curriculum. Individual differences among learners increase with age, so some way of accommodating self-paced learning is necessary. Adult learners tend to be more self-motivated, a trait which enhances self-paced learning. Perhaps most significant to adult learning situations is the establishment of an environment where the trainer is engaged in a spirit of inquiry *with* the trainee(s), rather than taking the role of the authority who is the fount of all knowledge. The self-esteem of the adult learner must be protected, and this is accomplished when an atmosphere of shared inquiry is promoted, and mistakes are disassociated from blame. One of the most useful things a trainer can do is to become familiar with adult learning theory and practice, before embarking on the design of a retraining program.

The design of a retraining program is also dependent on other variables, including the amount of resources the institution can afford to commit to such a program, and the number of employees that need to be trained. If a large number of employees need to be trained, group instruction involving audiovisual materials, particularly videotapes, and/or computer-assisted instruction (CAI) should be considered as a supplement to lecture. CAI is particularly valuable in that it allows trainees to move at their own pace, and learn from their mistakes in a non-threatening manner. At some point, however, the ratio of trainees to trainer will have to come down to 2 to 1 or 1 to 1, in order to teach the complex mix of details and decision-making that characterizes cataloging. It is often useful to allow trainees to work in pairs, trying to jointly solve problems before receiving feedback from the trainer. This can be done in breakout sessions, with the trainees meeting first as a larger group, and then scheduled for more exclusive sessions with the trainer to put into practice what they learned in the group session. If breakout sessions are intermixed with group instruction, it provides a change of pace and the necessary component of experiential learning.

The effectiveness of the training needs to be measured, and while tests can be constructed to do this, the best method is observing the trainee in an on-the-job situation while working with materials carefully chosen to present a variety of challenges. If a measurement of the trainee's incoming skills was done as part of a need assessment, a fairly accurate picture of the quality of the training can be assembled. The results from the testing phase should be examined to assess the progress of the trainee, and to provide feedback on the design and teaching methodology of the training program. Testing need not wait until the end of the training program; it is often more usefully interspersed within the training program to measure the trainee's mastery of one set of skills before moving on to a more difficult section. When designing the testing phase, it is important that the trainer remain cognizant of the need to protect the self-esteem of the trainee, and to conduct the test in as non-threatening a manner as is possible.

In smaller institutions it is possible to conduct retraining strictly on a one-on-one basis in a slightly more informal atmosphere. However, this does not mean that the steps of implementation of a retraining program outlined by Bales should be ignored or skipped. The same amount of care and thought needs to be given to a retraining program whether it involves one trainee or a dozen. The policy-makers and the staff involved in training need to decide the goals of the training program, what is to be taught and in what order, how much time is to be allotted to each section, how the training is to be implemented—and set this down on paper. Continuity of application is one of the most important skills of a cataloger, and this is no less important in training new catalogers. Lacking continuity in training, the quality of the institution's catalog will inevitably suffer.

THE RETRAINING PROCESS

When teaching cataloging, as in any other kind of training, a simple-to-difficult sequence needs to be followed. This would dictate, for example, that trainees be shielded from all knowledge of the serials format, until the trainer determines that they have developed the grounding in skills and the intestinal fortitude needed to tackle this Hydra-like cataloging monster. The unassuming monograph should be the starting point of any cataloging training program, with the initial emphasis placed upon the basic requirements of descriptive cataloging. Depending upon the outcome of the needs analysis of the trainee, the length of time needed by this portion of the training may vary considerably. As more and more MLS programs drop the requirement of a cataloging course for their graduates, the trainer may discover that it is necessary to teach the theoretical underpinnings of cataloging to his/her public service colleagues, as well as the nitty-gritty details. In other words, the "why" of cataloging must be taught as well as the "how." Without this theoretical background, the relationship of the various aspects of cataloging to each other will never be clearly understood, and the quality of the work will suffer.

In teaching the theoretical basis of cataloging, it is appropriate to introduce the cataloger's reference tools to the trainee, beginning with the second edition of the *Anglo-American Cataloging Rules* (AACR2). There are several published guides that help interpret AACR2, illustrating its rules with different cataloging problems that provide concrete examples for the novice.[17] Even more helpful are local manuals, developed in-house, that interpret AACR2 in light of local practices and priorities. Any library should have a written record of its local cataloging practices, but an augmented manual interpreting these practices is a necessity if the cataloging responsibilities are being expanded and decentralized.

When teaching the theory of descriptive cataloging special emphasis needs to be put on explaining the relationship between the body of the cataloging record and the access points. One of the advantages of OPACs over traditional card catalogs is their capacity for a substantially greater number of access points to a record. This advantage should be exploited by adding as many access points as possible to improve the retrieval rate of a record. However, it is a common mistake of novice catalogers to include access points in the form of added entries that are not explained in the body of the record. Thus the relationships between the different portions of a catalog record need to be carefully explained in the descriptive cataloging phase of training.

Selecting the proper access points to a record can be one of the most challenging facets of cataloging, and it is certainly the aspect that has the most impact on the library patron. Establishing main, added, and subject entries to a record usually involves a decision-making process, and the decisions can be anything but clear-cut.

Local practices that are set down in writing can aid in establishing a consistent pattern of access points. Such consistency is the hallmark of a good bibliographic database and will improve the performance of an OPAC.

Assigning appropriate subject headings is as much an art as a science. If cataloging duties are assigned to take advantage of subject specialties, as they are in some large libraries, improvement in the subject entries would likely result. For smaller libraries without the staff to allow for such specialization, a heavy reliance will need to be placed on the annual cumulation of *Library of Congress Subject Headings* (sometimes known as Big Red), supplemented by the *Subject Cataloging Manual,* the topical subject headings authority files found online in OCLC, and the changes to subject headings reported quarterly in the *Cataloging Service Bulletin.* Librarians with special subject expertise will also need to refer to these sources, but their in-depth knowledge will undoubtedly aid them in choosing from a vast array the most appropriate headings to assign to a record.

Once descriptive cataloging is thoroughly understood, it is time to show how it is encoded in the MARC format. Public service librarians with experience in searching WLN, RLIN or OCLC (perhaps via Firstsearch or EPIC) will no doubt move faster through this part of the learning process than librarians with little or no exposure to the major bibliographic utilities. The MARC coding may seem daunting at first, but when its connection to retrieval of records in the OPAC is explained, it is often a revelation to public service librarians and materially improves their retrieval rates in their library's OPACs. Understanding, for example, the role of the indicator that defines the number of spaces to ignore before indexing in the title field can aid a public services librarian in performing string searches in the OPAC. Coding in the fixed field is often used to limit searches by date or by the language of the material in the OPAC. Understanding these relationships will improve a librarian's performance in technical *and* public services.

In large libraries where cataloging may be divided up according to format and/or subject area, it may never be necessary for the cataloging trainee to learn to catalog any format other than monographs. Smaller libraries will probably not have that luxury, and the professional participating in cataloging will need to be introduced to other formats after becoming comfortable with monographs. A new format should probably not be introduced until the novice cataloger has successfully worked with monographs for six months. The process for introducing a new format should follow the same pattern established earlier; teaching and providing interpretation of AACR2 first, followed by the application of MARC coding practices. As the coding practices are not consistent between formats, the trainee should be encouraged to rely heavily on the OCLC or RLIN manual appropriate for the format, and not assume that coding as applied in the Books format can be carried over to other types of items. All things being equal, the next format taught after monographs should be Audiovisual Media, followed by Sound Recordings, Serials, Computer Files, and, if necessary, Archives and Manuscripts. This sequence would allow the trainee to follow the simple-to-difficult continuum described earlier.

The only major aspect of cataloging not yet touched upon is classification. The method for teaching this will depend on several variables: the classification system used, the organization of cataloging responsibilities in a library, and the extent of classification idiosyncrasies in a collection. For librarians who will have a wide range of cataloging responsibilities, the best tack may be to hold off the teaching of classification and allow the novice cataloger to work with adapting copy cataloging for local use, using the classification number supplied by CIP data or which is part of the record on the bibliographic utility. When the trainer is assured of the trainee's competence with the elements of descriptive cataloging, then it is time to turn attention to the teaching of classification. When cataloging responsibilities are arranged according to subject specialization, however, and only a portion of the classification scheme will be used, it is possible to teach it along with the rules of descriptive cataloging to the subject specialist. For the library using Dewey Decimal classification, the librarian cataloging may find it necessary to assign classification numbers to books that do not require original cataloging. If CIP information is absent and the MARC copy is member-supplied on OCLC, it is rare for a Dewey classification number to be present.

In many libraries the job of assigning the classification number in such a case is considered a duty that should fall to the professional cataloger.

Classification numbers from either scheme will certainly need to be assigned when doing original cataloging. The novice cataloger should be introduced to original cataloging in stages, first asked to provide only descriptive cataloging of the original piece, coded into the appropriate MARC format. Workforms arranged with the MARC format in mind are a useful tool. Normal or frequently used values can be filled in, and blanks placed where values still need to be applied to jog the memory. One word descriptions opposite the field tags also help orient the new cataloger. As mentioned earlier, in-house manuals describing local practices in relation to the MARC format are tremendously helpful. A two or three page local guide to a MARC format, tied to the OCLC or other utility's guide by citing the appropriate page numbers, can go a long way toward orienting and interpreting the MARC record. The Appendix contains a guide from the Dickinson College Library. Local practices may vary from format to format; not all libraries are willing or able to provide I-level cataloging for all formats. If a lesser standard is decided upon, the local manual needs to clearly spell out what the implications are of using the lesser standard. The issue of mandatory versus required versus optional fields in a format needs to be addressed, and a decision reached on what optional fields, if any, will be filled in when cataloging at a level below I.

When the new cataloger is comfortable with description in the MARC context, it is time to add the assignment of classification numbers to their responsibilities for original cataloging. The last level that needs to be added is authority control. Establishing subject authority has been discussed earlier. Establishing name authorities begins with the online authority file, and the proper method for searching this file needs to be taught. Even librarians experienced at searching for bibliographic copy will need training to properly search and interpret the online authority file. The new mnemonic form of authority records introduced in OCLC with the onset of PRISM helps in the interpretation of the authority format, but a local manual interpreting key values and discussing their application is still necessary. When a name is *not* found in the online authority file, procedures for establishing the correct form of the name need to be spelled out in local documentation. The public service librarian's greater familiarity with reference tools will stand him/her in good stead when establishing names and birth/death dates. This is a prime example of the synergistic effect of holistic librarianship, as the establishment of a name authority can bring both technical and public services skills into play. A name authority properly established, possibly with pseudonyms or other forms of the name cross-referenced (according to the capabilities of the OPAC), will directly influence the library patron's rate of retrieval from the OPAC. In a larger context, member cataloging contributed to a bibliographic utility with the best possible name authority established impacts on the quality of OPACs throughout the network, when members import that record for their own use.

QUALITY CONTROL

When cataloging responsibilities are being decentralized, whether into subject specialization or simply into a greater number of people with a more tenuous connection with the core of the Technical Services department, some thought needs to be given to the issue of quality control. To many administrators and uninitiated public service librarians, this issue is viewed as an irritating bugaboo, the product of compulsive personalities (alias catalogers) of little importance in the overall scheme of library work. This attitude is rather curious considering the crucial role the OPAC plays in the library. A $200 art book with a record that cannot be accessed easily due to poor cataloging is a waste of a library's resources by any standard. The concept of "garbage in, garbage out" applies to a library's OPAC as much as to any other type of database.

The dilemma is how to ensure a good level of quality control without investing a great deal of time and labor. First and foremost is to establish good communication between the new catalogers and more experienced cataloging staff. Encouraging consultation among staff will prevent mistakes, and is far more cost effective than any database clean-up project. For consultation to be an effective tool, the same atmosphere of openness and constructive correction that is needed in the training has to carry over into the regular work atmosphere.

Another strategy to aid in quality control is to stress methodical work habits for the new cataloger. If the training is presented in a well thought out, methodical way, it will go a long way toward establishing a productive, error-free approach to cataloging. This is not to say that there is a cast-iron approach which must be used by everyone. Rather, the new cataloger should be encouraged to find a way to approach the decision-making process of cataloging in a way that works for them, and then apply that same approach *every* time. Ideally, original cataloging should be scrutinized by another professional librarian before it is contributed to a national bibliographic utility or a local OPAC. The second pair of eyes looking at the workform on paper, or better still, on the screen before it is produced, must be willing to provide constructive correction if problems are found. Receiving this kind of feedback will do more to facilitate continued learning than any other mechanism.

Continuing education in cataloging is a necessity, not a frill. It should be the responsibility of the Head of Cataloging, or a designated experienced cataloger, to keep abreast of rule changes and hold regular update sessions for all cataloging staff. Such a responsibility should be recognized with release time and financial support to attend workshops and conferences. All cataloging staff should be encouraged to attend cataloging-related workshops outside of the library. The bibliographic utilities all offer training sessions, as do the major suppliers of OPACs. Local networks affiliated with OCLC offer workshops specific to each format, usually run by leading experts. Training offered by sources outside of the library can offer a fresh viewpoint and serve as a welcome adjunct to in-house training.

After all the retraining or cross-training is completed, what can the library and the newly retrained librarian expect? If the training is an experiment in cross-training, the librarian will find that the variety of duties generally leads to an increase in job satisfaction. More career options are open as a result of newly developed skills.

The risk-taking involved in retraining for a completely different assignment will help develop leadership skills. It is not hard to see that the cross-trained librarian will have an edge as an administrator, possessing the knowledge and experience of both the major branches of library work. Librarians who are cross-trained also have a unique insight into the strengths and weaknesses of an OPAC from both a public and technical services perspective. This insight makes them a valuable resource to evaluate new technologies as they arrive, and to help the library successfully migrate to new systems in the future that will be technically efficient and patron-friendly. Public service librarians with cataloging responsibilities are in a good position to help establish cataloging priorities that reflect patron needs. A public service perspective can prevent cataloging tunnel vision, where catalogers get bogged down in details and lose sight of the service goals of the library.

The library with a pool of cross-trained librarians will gain a more flexible work force, able to shift to cover changing priorities. The Penn State library has implemented a cross-training program, and reported that the change helped them in recruiting new personnel. "As a result, the Penn State libraries are implementing online information systems more responsive to user needs, offering a more exciting and challenging work environment, and improving service programs in a highly competitive electronic market place."[18] The new job descriptions offer a higher level of flexibility, variety, and autonomy. The job integration had not produced lower quality cataloging, made time management impossible, or led to the development of "mediocre generalists."[19]

Lastly, the patrons benefit from having a staff knowledgeable about the full range of library services. Patron service remains the goal, even in an era of shrinking budgets and runaway inflation of materials prices. "Libraries must develop a stronger sense of organizational coherence within and across functional and structural boundaries. Only then will we make the best and most efficient use of our resources—both human and material." [20] Making the most of human and material resources is what retraining is designed to accomplish.

APPENDIX

Guide to the Book Workform

The following notes are only guidelines; please refer to the OCLC Books Format Manual for more complete information about each field.

The monographs workform developed at Dickinson is meant to be easy to use and remember. The codes beside each variable field indicate that the information is:

M = *Mandatory* in the record

R = *Required* in the record if the information is readily obtainable from the piece in hand.

0 = *Optional* in the record (i.e., not required for I level cataloging)

Notes are given below for each field on the workform, in order to assist in cataloging books as consistently as possible.

NOTE—Fields printed in **Bold** type below appear on the monograph workform and are important for Dickinson. Fields printed in normal type may appear on an OCLC record and are listed below for information only.

FIXED FIELDS:

M Type: a = Usually "a," printed language material—system supplied.

M Bib lvl: m = *Always* m for monograph

M Govt pub: b = Not a government publication. See *Books Format* for various codes if it is.

M Lang: = A three letter code for the primary language of the text. See OCLC Language code list.

M Source: d = Not Library of Congress cataloging. Always use for original cataloging.

O Illus: a = illustrations. Blank for none. See *Books Format* for additional codes.

R Repr: b = Usually blank indicating that the work is not a reproduction in a format that cannot be read by the naked eye or in oversize print.

M Enc lvl: I = Always "I" for complete original cataloging.

M Conf pub: 0 = Not a conference publication; 1 = conference
publication.

R Ctry: = Country of publication. See OCLC code list.

M Dat tp: = See *Books Format* for details. The Date Type must
coordinate with the Fixed Fields dates and 260,
subfield c.

O F/B = 1st position, 1 = main entry is repeated in 245, 0 =
main entry is *not* repeated in 245.

O Indx: 0 = no index; 1, index present.

R Mod rec: b = Record not modified.

M Festschr: 0 = Not a festschrift; 1 = a festschrift.

O Cont: b = No specified nature of contents. See *Books Format*
for details.

M Desc: a = AACR 2.

O Int lvl: b = Not applicable; j = juvenile work.

M Dates: = Contains one or two dates as appropriate. Must
coordinate with Date Type and 260 subfield c. See
Books Format.

VARIABLE FIELDS:

R 010, LC Card no.:   Both indicators are blank. Subfield a contains
Library of Congress card number.

M 040, Cataloging source: #a = origin of cataloging,
#c = contributor of cataloging.
Therefore for original cataloging
at Dickinson: #a DKC #c DKC.

R 020, ISBN: Subfield a contains International Standard Book
Number. Input *without* dashes, e.g., 08193-0503-
0 is input as 0819305030.

R 041, Language: 2nd indicator, 1 = translation 0 = not a
translation; use for multiple languages,
including parallel texts.

O 086, Documents number: Used at Dickinson for both U.S.
and Pa. documents. (If the docu-
ment has been given a Dewey
number, do not use this field.)

O 09X, Call number: 092 = #a Dewey number #b Cutter number (eight characters only. Thereafter, use a comma separating each eight characters.) 099 = Non Dewey number. #a only, repeatable.

M 049, Holdings: #a DKCX. [ ] [ ]'s following DKCX are required by the OCLC print program to separate each line of no more than eight characters. Produce and Send, and Reformat. Insert #a's preceding "see also" references and #o's before notes. Update and Send. (See cataloging manual for details.)

R 1XX, Main entry: Personal, corporate, conference or uniform title main entry.

R 240, Uniform title: Supply for most musical works and translated works.

M 245, Title: 1st indicator 1; 2nd indicator 0-9 non filing characters. #a, title, #b, subtitle, #c remainder of title page description.

R 250, Edition: Supply from work itself. See manual for valid abbreviations.

M 260, Imprint: #a, place of publication, #b, publisher, #c date(s)

M 300, Collation: #a, pagination, #b, illustrations, #c, size. Automatic oversize q designation beginning at 28 cm. (See manual for details.)

O 5XX, Notes: See OCLC Book Format for details. Examples:

501, "With" note. Use only for works that were PUBLISHED together. Use 500 for institution or copy specific "with" notes that have value beyond the local institution. Use 590 for local "with" notes. See *OCLC Books Format* for complete information.

505, Contents notes: The first indicator specifies the type of Contents note: 0 = Complete contents, 1 = Incomplete contents, 2 = Partial contents. Separate entries with "—." We add contents when the work contains essays by different authors and is of an interdisciplinary nature, or in the field of literature. DO NOT do contents longer than 3 pages (unless you choose to do incomplete contents). Please leave out chapter or division titles; format like this: Title / T. Brown—Title / P. Smith. (Use first initial only and last name in DIRECT order.) Include a note in the book requesting that contents be done, showing the first two titles formatted as shown above. Think twice before requesting contents for works in a foreign language, as that slows down inputting considerably.

533, Microform reproduction: Use this field to describe a microform reproduction of a work originally published in paper.

R 6XX, Subject headings: Use LC headings only. Supply for all works except fiction and drama.

M 910, Whodunit, When and Anals: The format is Anals 10/26/86:al/sn or simply 10/16/86:al/sn if analytics are not involved. Note: the date *must* be the date the record is *produced* and the reviser should normally be a librarian *other* than the one who created the original record. Also in this field is included information on replacements (see p. 97).

NOTES

1.   Michael Gorman, "On Doing Away With Technical Services Departments," *American Libraries* 10 (July/August 1979): 435.

2.   James G. Neal, "The Evolving Public/Technical Services Relationship: New Opportunities for Staffing the Cataloging Function," in *Recruiting, Educating, and Training Cataloging Librarians: Solving the Problems*, eds. Sheila S. Intner and Janet Swan Hill (New York: Greenwood Press, 1989), 113. Neal reports that in a 1986 study conducted by the Resources and Technical Division of ALA over a three month period, 94 positions with cataloging responsibilities were identified in library job advertisements. Seven months after the initial posting, 56% of the jobs were still vacant, and 64% were either re-advertised or extended. The openings attracted fewer than 11 applicants in 41% of the cases. The latter statistic is corroborated anecdotally by D. Whitney Coe in his article *"Recruitment, A Positive Process"* which appeared in the same volume with Neal. Coe notes that 10 years ago a library could expect 75-100 applicants for a cataloging position; today the number ranges between 10 and 15 (p.60).

3.   Barton M. Clark, "Holistic Librarianship," *Library Personnel News* 3 (Fall 1989): 55-7.

4.   John M. Cohn, "Integrating Public and Technical Services: Management Issues for Academic Libraries," in *The Smaller Academic Library: a Management Handbook*, ed. Gerard B. McCabe (Westport, CT: Greenwood Press, 1988), 308.

5.   Dana C. Rooks, *Motivating Today's Library Staff: A Management Guide* (Phoenix: Oryx Press, 1988), 75.

6.   Hugh C. Atkinson, "The Impact of New Technology on Library Organizations," in *The Bowker Annual of Library and Book Trade Information*, 29th ed. (New York: R.R. Bowker, 1984), 112.

7.   Allen B. Veaner, *Academic Librarianship in a Transformational Age: Program, Politics, and Personnel* (Boston: G. K. Hall, 1990), 112.

8.   B. J. Busch, "Automation and the Integration of Public and Technical Services Functions," *RTSD Newsletter* 10 (March 1985): 25-26.

9.   Jane A. Rosenberg and Maureen Sullivan, comp. *Resource Notebook on Staff Development* (Washington, D.C.: Association of Research Libraries, 1983), 170-77, 182-92, 274-79.

10.   Ibid., 176.

11.   Eleanor Gossen, Frances Reynolds, Karina Ricker, and Helen Smirensky, "Forging New Communication Links in an Academic Library: a Cross-Training Experiment," *Journal of Academic Librarianship* 16 (March 1990): 21.

12.   Anne G. Lipow, "Training for Change: Staff Development in a New Age," in *Human Resources Management in Libraries*, ed. Gisela M. Webb (New York: Haworth Press, 1989), 95-6.

13.   Gillian McCombs, "Public and Technical Services: the Hidden Dialectic," *RQ* 28 (Winter 1988): 141.

14.   Thomas W. Leonhardt, "Recruiting Catalogers: Three Sets of Strategies," in *Recruiting, Educating, and Training Cataloging Librarians: Solving the Problems*, eds. Sheila S. Intner and Janet Swan Hill (New York: Greenwood Press, 1989), 230.

15.   Sheila S. Intner, "Ten Good Reasons Why Reference Librarians Would Make Good Catalogers," *Technicalities* 9 (January 1988): 15.

16.   Kathleen Bales, "The Role of Training in the Changing Cataloging Environment," in *Recruiting, Educating, and Training Cataloging Librarians: Solving the Problems*, eds. Sheila S. Intner and Janet Swan Hill (New York: Greenwood Press, 1989), 316-17.

17.   One example of a volume interpreting AACR2 is Margaret F. Maxwell's *Handbook for AACR2 1988 Revision: Explaining and Illustrating the Anglo-American Cataloging Rules* (Chicago: American Library Association, 1989). Jay Weitz' *Music Coding and Tagging: MARC Content Designation for Scores and Sound Recordings* (Lake Crystal, MN: Soldier Creek Press, 1990) serves a similar purpose in relation to two MARC formats.

18.   Neal, "Evolving Public/Technical Services Relationship," 118-19.

19.   Ibid.

20.   Cohn, "Integrating Public and Technical Services," 310.

Chapter 9

RETRAINING OF SUPPORT STAFF IN LIBRARIES

Jean Purnell

A majority of the current literature on the training of support staff (defined as paraprofessional, technical, or clerical positions) in libraries focuses on three aspects of training: orientation and training of new employees; designing programs to enhance and augment the skills of current staff; and training to promote adaptation to change, which, in the last 15 years, has usually involved the computerization of library functions. This literature does not significantly address the retraining of staff who have been reassigned to positions in other departments within the library organization, for example, an acquisitions clerk who has been reassigned to the circulation department. Personnel management literature has devoted more attention to retraining; however, this material has only recently begun to be associated with white-collar workers rather than with blue-collar workers and specific industries. Despite which working group is being studied, the common focus of these discussions on retraining is the need to develop training programs that "teach employees skills for different jobs within the same organization" and "teach employees skills for an automated job."[1]

Most support staff in libraries are not taught "skills for different jobs within the same organization," but only those skills needed to perform the specific tasks of their individual positions. Retraining in libraries does not occur, therefore, until after a staff member is transferred into a new position. This chapter examines the factors that affect the retraining of library staff, as viewed from the perspective of the trainers and employees involved, with a focus on ways to ensure that the retraining period is successful. A linkage between an ongoing staff development program and retraining is also explored as a creative option for library managers planning for effective utilization of human resources. Information regarding the opinions and attitudes of trainers and employees involved in retraining was gathered through a study (including selective interviewing) of eleven employees and their trainers, both past and present, who in the last ten years were retrained in new assignments at University of the Pacific (UOP) Libraries. Staff size at the UOP Libraries, which consists of a central library with one branch, has averaged twelve faculty and nineteen support staff positions over the last ten years.

STAFF TRANSFER AND RETRAINING

Staff transfer in libraries may occur for a variety of reasons, which may be perceived as either beneficial or detrimental to the employee, but usually beneficial to the organization. Employees may be selected for vacant positions that have been advertised; their selection may involve a promotion to a higher rank or simply a lateral move within the organization. This type of change is logically beneficial for both the individual and the organization, particularly because both the employee and department freely choose to make the change. Staff transfers may also be a result of a necessary reallocation of staff resources, forced by budget cuts, unfilled positions, or the decline or growth of programs. Organizational restructuring of a library may result in the reassignment of a staff member from one department to another, perhaps with the elimination or merging of departments. These types of reassignment are usually made on the basis of solving organizational problems. Selection of staff for reassignment is undertaken with the hope of matching employee skills to the requirements of the position, and of employee satisfaction with the new position, but this is not always the case. Reassigned employees may resent the change and feel that their past contributions to the library have been devalued. Staff transfers may occur as a result of poor performance in a department, or lack of required skills for a certain type of work. This change may be perceived by the employee in two ways: a beneficial, new opportunity, or a form of punishment.

When seen simply as the necessary result of staff reassignment, retraining may appear to be occurring more now than ever before. The 1990s are likely to be remembered by many in educational institutions as the decade of downsizing, a time when budgetary cutbacks in public and private institutions not only lowered the ceiling on libraries' acquisition of materials but also effectively reduced the size of faculty and staff through retirement incentive programs, staff attrition, and, when necessary, layoffs. Academic libraries have been no exception to this trend, and the retraining of staff will therefore become of even greater interest to library managers who are just now making the difficult decisions about how to reallocate the remaining staff to fulfill essential services. Turnover in the top levels of library administration may also bring organizational restructuring, increasing the need to retrain support staff. At the UOP Libraries, at least eight employees out of a total of nineteen support staff positions were reassigned to new positions. Of these, one employee was reassigned twice within a single year, and three others were promoted to new positions. The sheer weight of these numbers, probably not atypical for other libraries experiencing internal or external influences similar to those described above, should convince managers that the retraining of reassigned employees is an issue that needs to be addressed, not only after the transfer occurs, but in the design of ongoing staff training and development programs.

FACTORS AFFECTING RETRAINING

Degree of Similarity or Contrast Between Positions

Retraining of library staff is affected by the degree of similarity or contrast between the skills required to perform the tasks of the previous and new positions. In some cases examined at the UOP Libraries, the previous and new position assignments were similar, such as a clerk in the Reference Department who became a clerk in Interlibrary Loan. The tasks involved in these two positions shared skill requirements of understanding bibliographic information, locating library materials, searching a national bibliographic database, and clerical handling of forms and filing. Knowledge acquired in the previous position could be applied to the performance of many aspects of the new job. In other cases, the new position shared little in common with the old, such as a supervisor in a photocopy office who was reassigned as a circulation clerk or a cataloger who became an acquisitions supervisor and vendor contact. In the first case, the photocopy supervisor had no knowledge of library systems of organization such as the Library of Congress classification system or location and shelving of library materials. In the second case, the cataloger, while knowledgeable of AACR2 cataloging rules, MARC formats, and RLIN searching and inputting procedures, was inexperienced in the language of acquisitions, claims, invoices, and in handling salespersons. In these two situations, the employee brought less relevant experience to the new position. Successful retraining, therefore, depended more on the employee's potential skills and adaptability. It is probably unlikely, however, that when these two employees were originally hired, the ability to develop new skills or adaptability in the face of change were highly emphasized as requirements of the positions.

Reasons for Staff Reassignment

The various reasons for staff reassignment, such as promotion or transfer, play an important factor in determining the attitude of both employee and trainer (or supervisor) toward retraining. In the eleven examples studied, eight of the eleven reassigned employees filled vacant positions; one of these vacancies occurred because of another reassignment; three of the eight vacancies were filled by promotion from within. The remaining three employees joined departments as an additional staff member. Library managers' decisions to reassign these eleven employees were based on one or more of the following reasons:

1. Growth of a department required additional staff
2. A critical vacancy occurred when staff positions were frozen campus-wide
3. Simultaneous merging and elimination of departments caused the elimination of an employee's previous responsibilities
4. Employee did not have enough work to do in previous position
5. Employee promoted to new position
6. Employee showed potential or had skills not being realized in previous position
7. Employee performance not meeting expectations of the department

Supervisors' Attitudes

While the new supervisors and/or trainers of these reassigned or promoted employees, for the most part, had positive attitudes about working with the new employees, they experienced similar problems in the training process, often caused by their lack of participation (and lack of participation by the employee) in choosing the new employee. Supervisors participated fully in recruiting for the three positions filled by promotion. In most of the other cases, however, the supervisor had some advance knowledge that the reassignment was going to take place, but did not make the actual decision. Decisions were usually made by the library administration with input from the supervisor or department head as to whether the reassignment would be beneficial for the department. Some trainers were skeptical that the new employee would be happy in the new position and felt that the employee's feelings about the transfer cast a potentially negative shadow over the transition. While glad to have positions filled, supervisors were frustrated when reassigned employees did not always immediately have the skills required for the new positions and lacked experience that other potential applicants might have had. Some trainers working with these employees found that departmental productivity during the training period was lower than expected, and that patience was required to allow for an adequate period of time required by the employee to become competent in the new routines.

The quality of the training reassigned employees received also varied according to the amount of time trainers felt was necessary to invest in these new employees. In more than one case, supervisors and employees described the initial training as limited to task-specific assignments rather than any organized orientation to departmental tasks and routines. In these cases, whether intentionally or not, the assumption was made that the employees already had some knowledge of the general functions of the department and library and therefore did not require the same intensive orientation as would be prepared for a new hire. Employees bringing the least relevant experience to their new positions received the most extensive orientation and training, both in content and duration.

Employees' Attitudes

As with the trainers, employees being retrained in new assignments shared common experiences and attitudes. Except for those who actually applied for a vacant position, almost all employees stated that they had not been personally consulted or given much advance notice regarding the reassignment to a new position. None had received any specific training that would have prepared them for their subsequent reassignment. Several were removed from positions that were seen by management as less than a full workload or less vital to library functions than the position they assumed. Several employees confided that they felt devalued or manipulated in the process, and that despite receiving positive performance evaluations, they viewed the reassignment as a subtle message conveying that their past contributions to the library were insignificant. Rarely was a reassignment accompanied with an increase in salary or upgrade in job rank. Some employees openly expressed feelings of inadequacy, frustration at not knowing what they were doing in their first few weeks at the new job, or fear that they would not be able to perform the job well. Reassigned employees did not view themselves as new hires, but, often like their trainers, felt that they were expected to adapt quickly to basic tasks and routines. Some were removed from comfortable tasks they had performed for many years. Some felt deprived of familiar surroundings and longtime departmental colleagues. Nonetheless, despite undercurrents of resentment, most employees showed loyalty to the library and a positive attitude and enthusiasm toward the new activities. Employees that eventually left the library could cite other reasons in addition to or separate from the reassignment as factors for their resignation.

DESIGNING A RETRAINING PROGRAM

The careful design of a training and development program that includes retraining of support staff must take into account the fact that while reassignment can be seen as a potential development opportunity for a current employee, it may also be accompanied by more negative aspects than the hiring and training of a new employee. A retraining program may be different from the established program for new hires in several ways, but it should not be automatically abbreviated in content or duration. The trainer should not make assumptions about the abilities or knowledge of the employee, nor deprive the employee of an adequate training period simply because he/she has previous experience at the library.

The design of a retraining program after staff reassignment should include the following steps for the trainer. First, the trainer should attempt to establish a sense of honest and open rapport with the employee within a short period of time, especially if the reassignment has been announced and implemented on short notice. The trainer should, as much as possible, be aware of the reasons for reassignment, and be willing to listen and respond to the employee's feelings about the change of assignment. This willingness may help to overcome any negative feelings or resentment the employee may have toward the new supervisor or assignment. The supervisor should be able to articulate the goals of the library administration, especially if the reassignment reflects a restructuring of the organization or is based on the decline or growth of library programs.

Second, the trainer should determine the individual's training needs through a systematic assessment of the individual's abilities and the requirements of the new position. The importance of this task lies in discovering the "real training needs," described by John Kupersmith as that gap between what the employee knows and what he/she needs to know in order to do his/her job effectively.[2] The training needs assessment should be based on data gained from an examination of the employee's past experience, including performance reviews; from interviews with the employee and his/her past supervisors; and through testing where the employee is encouraged to demonstrate his/her abilities.

Third, the trainer should identify the performance objectives and communicate these to the staff member at the outset of training. An evaluation of the needs assessment will allow the trainer to develop performance objectives that are specific to the employee, rather than the position. Performance objectives should be simply worded, and state what the employee will be able to do after training. The needs assessment may also allow the trainer to eliminate certain aspects of training in areas where the employee's skills are already developed.

The content of a retraining program should not omit a general orientation to the department or the function of the position. Employees at the UOP Libraries cited a general orientation to the new position and department as a frequently missing ingredient in their training programs, while trainers felt that certain basic information of this type was likely to be commonly known. Mistaken assumptions can be avoided if trainers provide the same general orientation to the department and position in retraining as for a new hire. This would give some longtime employees a new opportunity to learn information about the library not shared in their training at the time of first employment. Supervisors should take nothing for granted and, as Sheila Creth states, "prepare training plans for all new staff no matter what the person's experience or background, and for staff with new assignments."[3]

The last step in preparation for retraining is the development of a proposed timetable for the training. Trainers should avoid giving the impression that the employee should learn more quickly than a new hire; care should be taken to avoid creating unrealistic expectations or increased pressure on the employee to be immediately successful in the performance of new tasks. The tone of retraining should emphasize a positive belief that the employee can gain necessary skills. Support from the supervisor and colleagues in giving positive feedback can be instrumental in dispelling fears of inadequacy or feelings of frustration during the training period. A timetable for evaluation of progress toward meeting performance objectives should also be developed and clearly communicated. Periodic evaluation of the employee's progress will naturally result in readjustments of the timetable or a revision of the performance objectives.

Support staff may benefit by attending classes or workshops that teach skills or knowledge needed to work with automated systems, networks, software, skills to handle customers or work with vendors, supervisory skills, or any of a variety of subjects relevant to support staff positions. On the other hand, on the job experiential learning, applying learned knowledge immediately by practicing job tasks, not only increases the retention of knowledge, but has special value as a training methodology for the reassigned employee: establishing as quickly as possible a measure of comfort with basic aspects of the job. These employees often experience discomfort associated with the loss of the routine of the previous assignment and are anxious to fit in to the new position as quickly as possible. Trainers can help by building on the employee's previous skills whenever possible, and allowing new challenges to be approached gradually in the training timetable.

Except in very large library organizations, the employee being retrained is likely to know his/her new colleagues and supervisor and have varying degrees of familiarity with the new surroundings. This familiarity can help provide a measure of comfort to the employee going through the transition period. It can also produce awkwardness when employees work closely together that have not previously had much in common. When possible the involvement of colleagues in the retraining program should be encouraged as an aid toward helping to build supportive work relationships.

Mentor relationships, not only between supervisor and employee, but also between peers, can help to establish the concept that support and assistance in retraining is available through collegial networking as well as from one's supervisor. The new employee can eventually become a trainer for others in the department, as expertise is mutually recognized and shared.

STAFF DEVELOPMENT THROUGH RETRAINING

The need for library managers to develop programs to keep their employees' skills current is not a new challenge, yet the degree to which managers are successful varies widely. A dim view is voiced by Creth, who states, "I am not certain that as a profession we are doing much better in addressing staff development either on a daily basis in specific skills training or regarding major institutional change."[4] Training programs are time-consuming to design and implement, and may require significant financial investment to maintain. Unfortunately, libraries often invest more time and funds in development programs for professionals to carry out and present research than in programs to enhance the skills of support staff, despite the fact that the support staff is the library's most stable human resource. As Stephen B. Wehrenberg writes regarding "Training Megatrends," managers and trainers must "take stock of the current skill pool, determine what pool of skills will be needed in the future, and develop a plan to cross-train and retrain to get there."[5] Cross-training or staff exchange programs are already being used by some libraries, such as Stanford University Libraries, as a type of staff development. This involves having a staff member apply to work in another department for an extended period of time, ranging from six months to two years, but eventually returning to the original assignment. The weekly allotment of a staff member's time to the exchange varies from a few hours to full-time.[6] The benefit of such a program is to increase the number of skills that individual employees have, creating a "reserve" of potential should the possibility of promotion or reassignment arise in the future. As the computerization of libraries and information changes the skills required of our current staff, and with opportunities for reassignment of staff likely to increase in the near future, libraries with such a program of retraining through cross-training will be well-positioned to make decisions that are beneficial for both the employee and organization. The retraining of reassigned support staff, in the context of such a program, would be merely the next logical step in staff development. While a program involving the temporary full-time reassignment of support staff may be more difficult to maintain in a small library than a large library, a structured program of cross-training, where employees do not simply attend the occasional skills workshop, but actually get to practice skills learned on the job by working in other departments or areas for at least a few hours per week, will be a wise investment in developing that "pool of skills" needed to maintain library services in the future. Retraining as part of a structured staff development program also helps identify potential career employees who are likely to be considered for promotion or new assignments in the future.

THE LIBRARY MANAGER'S ROLE

Employees and supervisors with experience in retraining of support staff can provide helpful insight for library managers into what makes the retraining process a successful transition or a difficult situation. The problems encountered by trainers and employees were often related primarily to the abruptness of the transition for the employee, and secondarily, to the reason for the reassignment. Attitudes toward retraining were sometimes colored by negative feelings about the new position, and frustration occasionally surfaced on the part of both trainer and employee when the employee's skills or experience did not closely compare with the new position. Managers would be well-advised to consider the benefits of additional consultation with the employee and supervisor involved before making decisions regarding reassignment, and whenever possible, involve support staff in training to enhance present skills prior to promotion or transfer. Retraining of employees could then be promoted as a developmental activity, in which employees are selected for training in order to accept new or increased responsibilities, and given support to respond positively, rather than with resentment, to change.

NOTES

1.   Margaret Magnus, "Training Futures," *Personnel Journal*, May 1986, 63, 66.
2.   John Kupersmith, "Preparing Training Needs Assessments," Training Skills Institute, (Washington, DC Association of Research Libraries Office of Management Studies, 1991), workshop materials.
3.   Sheila Creth, "Staff Development: Where Do We Go From Here?" *Library Administration & Management* 4, no.3 (Summer 1990): 132.
4.   Creth, 131.
5.   Steven B. Wehrenberg, "Training Megatrends," *Personnel Journal*, April 1983, 279.
6.   *Internships in ARL Libraries*, Spec Kit, no. 79 (Washington, DC: Association of Research Libraries Office of Management Studies, 1981), flyer. Of the 73 ARL members responding to the survey, 15 had staff exchange programs.

REFERENCES

Creth, Sheila. "Staff Development: Where Do We Go From Here?" *Library Administration & Management 4*, no. 3(Summer 1990): 131-132.
Internships in ARL Libraries. Spec Kit, no. 79. Washington, DC: Association of Research Libraries Office of Management Studies, 1981.
Kupersmith, John. "Preparing Training Needs Assessments," Training Skills Institute. Washington, DC: Association of Research Libraries Office of Management Studies, 1991. Workshop materials.
Magnus, Margaret. "Training Futures." *Personnel Journal*, May 1986, 60-71.
Wehrenberg, Steven B. "Training Megatrends." *Personnel Journal*, April 1983, 279-280.

STAFF DEVELOPMENT

Chapter 10

CREATIVITY TRAINING IN ACADEMIC LIBRARIES

Susan P. Besemer

INTRODUCTION

When I reached Hannelore Rader by telephone one sun-washed October afternoon, to talk to her about creativity in libraries, she was preparing for a consulting trip to China. "Creativity training?" she asked. "We found it was necessary to train our staff to solve problems more creatively as we began implementing our new library organizational structure, when I came to Cleveland State in 1987." In my conversation with Ms. Rader, we shared our interest in team management, and discussed how necessary creative approaches are to academic library work in the 1990s and into the 21st century.[1] Her enthusiasm, energy, and impassioned commitment to improved services for patrons and to professional and staff development became clear. For Hannelore, as for many other academic library managers, creativity training was a step along the path to another goal.

The link between teamwork and developing staff creativity was also made in an interesting article by Katherine W. Hawkins.[2] Ms. Hawkins explicitly states the value of a team management orientation in encouraging the creativity which is needed to address the challenges facing libraries today.

Creativity training is certainly not a commonplace staff development activity in libraries. Generally, it takes place only when library managers see the need to try alternative approaches to solving problems because traditional solutions sometimes no longer fit the environments in which we presently operate.

The need for creativity in librarianship has been acknowledged and demonstrated in the work of a few outstanding individuals from the early days of our profession. Other needs to preserve order and to meet traditional service expectations have not always encouraged creative practices. Charles Clarence Williamson of Columbia stated in 1943, in a collection of papers celebrating the fiftieth anniversary of the University of Illinois Library School, that he was "not at all sure that we are doing a better job of training creative librarians than did our pioneering predecessors of fifty years ago."[3] This concern was reiterated nearly forty years later in another commemorative anniversary publication, this time for the School of Library Science at The University of North Carolina at Chapel Hill. David Kaser, of Indiana University, wrote persuasively of the need for creativity in performing the research of the discipline, as well as in the practice of librarianship.[4]

There is a challenging array of problems as well as opportunities to learn and grow which present themselves to modern academic librarians. There are demands for new services without additional staff, needs to automate library operations or to migrate from one automated system to another, the necessity to cope with unbridled inflation in the costs of serials and other materials; and there is our desire to implement programs for underserved patrons and for information literacy. How are we to achieve these goals with limited resources? That, indeed, is the question for the nineties!

Creativity training in academic libraries can help library managers empower their staffs through encouraging them to look to their own collective experience and imagination to solve the problems that present themselves in today's dynamic library environment. Although creativity training is fun, it is not just for fun. By using structured approaches to solving problems, while incorporating the mind-expanding techniques of divergent thinking, solutions present themselves which of their own energy impel the staff to implementation. Such efforts validate the often extensive experience and intellectual strength of library faculty and staff. While other resources may be curtailed, and while staff size may be limited, our native human creativity is without bounds. The intellectual and creative ability of staff to cope with difficult circumstances is beyond measure. In fact, our ability to achieve quality breakthroughs, by looking with new insights at the problems we face, may be challenged and encouraged to grow in less than happy circumstances.

How and where can library staffs learn the techniques of openmindedness that will allow them to become more effective and productive problem solvers? This is the basic question that this chapter will address. We'll consider what one library school professor did to train the students entering our ranks to solve problems creatively, then look at what can be done in the workplace, and at what opportunities exist for creativity training sponsored by professional organizations both inside and outside the library and information science field. The chapter will close with a description of the stages of a typical problem-solving session which shows how a structured approach to problem solving can address current problems. The section is designed to highlight the structure and techniques of a commonly taught problem-solving method, the Osborn-Parnes Creative Problem-Solving Process.

PRE-SERVICE TRAINING

It may be that creative thinking and behavior are skills which are needed in academic libraries, but nowadays few library schools directly address the need for creativity. They have all that they can do to teach the theoretical and practical skills of our profession, including extensive bibliography and reference courses, management and personnel courses, and courses utilizing computing applications, without offering courses or even sections of courses that deal with techniques for looking for and implementing new ideas, no matter how valuable such courses might be.

One library school professor did try it, however. An interesting adventure into creativity training and the teaching of problem solving was made at Simmons College in the 1970s. Dr. A. J. Anderson was, in the late sixties, Director of the Andover,

Massachusetts Public Library. A community member and library user spoke to Anderson about the value and benefits of an innovative problem-solving method called Synectics, which was attracting interest in the Boston area.[5] Dr. Anderson went on to become a trained leader in the Synectics process, and taught the metaphorical methodology to school and community groups, eventually using it in his "Service to Adults" course at Simmons. Although Professor Anderson no longer runs Synectics sessions in his Simmons classes, he maintained that his experience with this problem-solving methodology "dated a new era in my life."[6]

Synectics techniques are very structured in format, but their content is fanciful because the sessions make extensive use of metaphor and imagination. Anderson asserted that his experience with creativity training has allowed his mind to "fly with wild abandon" during the divergent stages of the creative process.[7]

Such testimonials to the liberating qualities of creativity training are not unusual. The popular press often runs articles about how businesses are remaining competitive through training that strengthens the company's level of innovation and creativity.[8, 9] A recent article in *U.S. News and World Report* states that "Creativity has become another hot button in the executive suite, corporate America's reaction to global competition and runaway technology. Nearly 1 company in 3 now offers 'creativity training' to its employees."[10]

The recent interest in information literacy and critical thinking skills in library instruction is linked very closely to problem solving. Students need to know how to find new ideas to be able to locate information and to develop successful information-seeking strategies. It is hoped that more schools of library and information science will offer creativity training to help emerging librarians cope more resourcefully with the rapid pace of change in our society, a fact which libraries, like other cultural entities, cannot escape.

WORKPLACE TRAINING SESSIONS

Staff development and training take many forms, some of which have been discussed in other chapters. Any kind of library training may involve bringing an outside expert to the library to share technical information with staff, or, as in the case of creativity training, to stimulate consideration of the question of innovation and openness to new ideas. Inviting a facilitator or trainer to the library to consult with management and staff to plan and present training sessions can pay off in increased motivation to cope with change, in the willingness to "own" the problems that confront us, and in developing skills that provide solutions to the problems. In fact, Susan Jurow, of the Office of Management Services at the Association of Research Libraries, stated recently that the workplace is the most successful venue for the creativity training sessions that ARL offers.[11] Sessions at M.I.T. and Columbia were extremely productive and involving, Jurow noted.

Sheila Creth made the case for staff developing the "ownership" of problems in the workplace. She stated very convincingly in her 1986 publication for the American Library Association that the corporate culture and the socialization of employees becomes very important when change is introduced into the library.

> Libraries are full of valuable and valued traditions, but many of these are being challenged and altered; staff are often not prepared to let go of old ways and thus to accept new approaches or requirements. It is through the training process that supervisors can assist staff in cultivating an attitude that will enable them to work effectively.[12]

Consultants both from within the profession and those from business or education can assist managers by bringing special expertise to this area which has not yet been thoroughly explored in libraries. Before a consultant or facilitator is brought in, it may be beneficial to encourage reading on the topic and develop informal leaders who may learn about the techniques and processes of creative problem solving. Without preparing staff, it is possible that resistance can be great because the techniques seem to be so different from those normally used in the academic environment. Some suggestions for reading and viewing appear in the references for this chapter, while others may be found in the literature of business, under the rubric "Innovation Training."

Techniques that allow librarians to gain perspective and new insights into troubling situations are sometimes received with such gratitude that the successful practitioner becomes an enthusiast. A few voices in the library literature have called for more use of creative techniques,[13, 14] but there is much room for growth. Librarians' enthusiasm for these techniques has yet to be fully tapped, but is definitely growing. Susan Jurow indicated that now the ARL receives more specific requests for creativity training than for any other single topic.[15] She agreed with other authors who find such training especially worthwhile under difficult fiscal circumstances. "We need this now," she asserted.

Still, creativity training is viewed by some with skepticism. Perhaps the fears that keep individuals from performing their creative best are magnified when training is institutionalized. When such well-regarded authorities as Anderson and Jurow cite the usefulness of creativity in problem solving we might do well to consider their comments. In fact, Anderson has stated that, although the Synectics techniques are highly original and metaphorical, few in his classes or instruction sessions have resisted trying them.[16] Without specifically discussing Synectics, Anderson developed a model for problem solving in his text *Problems in Library Management.*[17]

Larger libraries may have budgets that allow consultants or trainers to be brought in, but many other library managers may have to be creative just to get the training for their staffs! We have long practiced continuing growth through our own reading of the library literature. Certainly, using that method with the literature of creativity training will help both the library management team and the library faculty and staff lay the groundwork, through the intellectual process of reading and study.

Renting or borrowing a videocassette on the subject of problem solving can be a good way to set the stage for future training sessions. A well-researched resource like *Creative Problem Solving: How to Get Better Ideas* can open the topic in an positive, action-oriented mode.[18]

Thinking creatively is a skill that takes practice, and this skill requires a more physically involving approach than other more academic or intellectual practices take. How can we get that practice? Invite a librarian from a neighboring library or a regional center to lead your staff through the steps of the process. She or he may be able to provide just enough distance from your problems to avoid shutting down the pathways to new ideas. Later, you may be invited to play that role for another group. Our problems are always shared, but our unique insights can help others get a new direction toward new solutions.

Most business departments in academic institutions have professors who have led brainstorming or other problem-solving sessions. These may include such techniques as Kepner-Tregoe, Value Engineering, Delphi Method or Nominal Group Technique.[19] A few library publications mention brainstorming and other related techniques. Unfortunately, some authors[20] treat the matter so superficially that people exposed to these materials are misled about the skills required and the possible benefits of the techniques.

Fortunately, there are many in higher education who are knowledgeable about divergent thinking techniques. Departments or schools of education have likely taught Creative Problem Solving (CPS) or another problem-solving method like Synectics.[21] By asking a colleague's assistance, you can gain an ally in the department, and gain new insights into your problems, as well. The colleague's students may also help by joining you in a brainstorming session. How infrequently we make use of the fresh ideas of our patrons, when looking for ideas for problems that involve them! Another opportunity to reach out to our patron audience exists through the CPS process.

TRAINING OFFERED AT OTHER SITES

It could also be beneficial to send a member of the library faculty to receive training at a professional conference or at a training center where creativity and innovation strategies are taught. Checking through a recent issue of Training magazine[22] will reveal several which might be useful, although possibly costly. The Association of Research Libraries offers creativity training through their Office of Management Services programs, both in public programs and in invited seminars on site; while ACRL has also offered workshops in creativity from time to time.[23]

One of the best-known opportunities for learning more about doing creative problem solving from a practical viewpoint is the Creative Problem Solving Institute, offered in Buffalo by the Creative Education Foundation for more than 40 years. Each summer, the Institute offers training to hundreds of attendees from varied professions and from many countries in groups that capitalize on this diversity.

Other opportunities for innovation training exist at the Center for Creative Leadership, the Center for Studies in Creativity, SES Associates (Synectics Education Systems), and Synectics, Inc. Many academic departments and continuing education divisions of universities around the country and around the world also offer creativity training.[24]

THE CREATIVE PROBLEM-SOLVING PROCESS

If getting away or having someone help with the training process is truly impossible, it may be a necessary and still viable alternative to use books and other resources to learn a creative problem-solving process. The following suggests one approach to problem-solving that might be helpful.

Although everyone agrees that scientists, engineers, artists and librarians go through a creative process when coming up with new and useful ideas, there is not one universally agreed-upon naming and sequencing for the steps or stages involved in the process. Even the notion that there are steps and stages in the process is resisted by some. When it is working well, the creative process just flows, but when ideas are blocked, a formal, structured process can be fruitful in shaking loose the ideas.

Several well-known articulations of the process exist. One principle of any formulation of the creative process is the notion of keeping open one's awareness to new ideas. This openness may be natural, often seen in novices to a field, or in children. But when dealing with adults, especially adult experts, one soon realizes that they feel strongly the imperatives of past experience, and "what works here."

Because of the danger of shutting off new ideas due to prior experience and group pressures to maintain the status quo, all structured problem solving approaches utilize techniques that allow the participants to temporarily step aside from their day-to-day viewpoints and adopt, for a predetermined time, a fresh perspective, often called "divergent thinking." [25]

The methods used to provide this objectivity include such techniques as brainstorming, fantasy excursions, the use of remote associates or "force fit." [26] Another divergent technique involves working with another person who deliberately asks questions "from left field" or guides the partner through checklists of idea-spurring questions.

While the steps in various problem-solving methods vary, most are similar to the Wallas method, first articulated in 1926. The steps he outlined were "preparation, incubation, illumination, verification." [27] The importance of "incubation" suggests the need to deliberately step away from the problem at some point and let the problem rest. Because of the intense focus that most really sticky problems receive, the problem solver often gets stuck in a rut that keeps him or her from seeing a truly simple fact of the problem that may contain the seed of a solution. Being able to set the problem aside by allowing the problem solver to "incubate" is a critical part of any problem-solving method.

Another important feature of successful problem solving sessions involves an emphasis on "solving the right problem." One of the most common traps of conventional problem-solving techniques is rushing to the solution before all aspects of the problem are thoroughly explored. Kaser cited this as a weakness in the research in librarianship. [28] The desire to remove oneself from the ambiguity of not knowing what to do can be so frightening and debilitating that problem solvers often anxiously grab for solutions to their pressing problems one idea at a time, trying and failing with first one option, then another. A more productive approach is to immerse oneself thoroughly in all aspects of the problem, to explore it from as many points of view as possible and with other people if feasible, then to generate many different formulations of the problem, in an attempt to find out what is "the real problem." There may be many real problems implicit in the situation, but they cannot all be addressed at once. Hopefully, by deciding which problem, or which aspect of the problem, the problem solver is going to address first, he or she may choose to work on an easy or an important aspect of the problem, while remembering that many other problems reside in the original situation.

THE OSBORN-PARNES MODEL

One method commonly used with success is called the Osborn-Parnes model of Creative Problem Solving (CPS). This strategy was based on the creative idea generating techniques of Buffalo advertising executive Alex Osborn, of Batten, Barton, Durstine, and Osborn, Inc. While practicing his craft, Osborn developed the widely known technique called "brainstorming."[29] Osborn's technique, developed and taught by Dr. Sidney J. Parnes, used the conscious alternation of divergent and convergent thinking to present new insights through divergent methods while maintaining a hold in reality by constantly bringing problem solvers back to earth through convergent thinking.[30]

There are five stages in this process starting with an undefined and ambiguous "Mess." How well we recognize the aptness of this term. Without definition or form, the problem looms before us, urging anxious thoughts about how to "fix" the situation. The stages of the Creative Problem-Solving process are called *Fact Finding, Problem Finding, Idea Finding, Solution Finding,* and *Acceptance Finding.*

The first stage of the CPS process is *Fact Finding.* As was stated earlier, Fact Finding involves immersing oneself in the problem to become as thoroughly knowledgeable about the parameters of the problem as possible, realizing that the attitudes and perceptions of those in the problematic situation are as much "facts" of the problem as are the other more objective details of the scenario.

Problem Finding is the second stage. This activity consists of making numerous, varied, written formulations of statements of the problem. In each case, a conventional way of stating the problem is used which suggests the divergence of the upcoming step. Problem statements are generally formulated along this model: "In what ways might we...?" or "How to..." For example, we might say "In what ways might we keep students from ripping out pages from journal articles?" Or we might say, "How to keep periodical issues safe." In these two simple problem statements we can see the difference in solutions that may evolve from each of the alternatives. Each of these two formulations leads easily to the next stage of the process, Idea Finding.

In the third stage, *Idea Finding*, great divergence is sought. Here fantasy trips might ask how librarians on Mars might solve the problem, how children would solve it, or what ideas the Governor might have to address the problem. Since many of these formulations are a bit strange, problem solvers frequently have fun with this stage and become comfortable enough with each other and with the process to simply let the zany ideas roll.

Brainstorming, a technique which is familiar to many, puts a premium on divergent thinking. Four guidelines help make brainstorming effective. Group participants need to remember to *Defer Judgment*, realizing that the time for judging the ideas will come later in the process. Participants are encouraged to *Build on the Ideas of Others*, for often an idea proposed by one person can be greatly enhanced by elaboration proposed by another person. *The Wilder the Better* is another motto for brainstorming. It is said that it is easier to tame a wild idea than to breathe life into an old, tired idea.

The fourth guideline for brainstorming is sometimes difficult for problem solvers to understand. The guideline states that one should strive for *Quantity, Not Quality*. This injunction is so opposite to everything that we have been taught in school that many find the concept somewhat ridiculous. However, it is the very emphasis on quality that has shut down our imaginations to the possibilities that our creative minds can generate.

If we insist on quality in every idea that we allow ourselves to imagine, we may find the path to new ideas grows more and more narrow as we grow older and more expert in our field. When that path narrows to a rut, we may recognize the need to open up the pathway again with structured creativity techniques.

It may also be of interest to realize that psychologists who treat writers and scholars who suffer from writer's block often suggest that those so afflicted pursue a regular writing program that does not concern itself with the quality of the product. The effort and the practice of writing, without regard to quality, helps blocked writers to get their ideas flowing again.[31]

The fourth part of the Creative Problem-Solving process, *Solution Finding*, is an essentially convergent stage, although there are ways of generating divergence even here. Ideas proposed during Idea Finding are evaluated after participants have generated a list of criteria or benchmarks that will be used to test the merits of the ideas. It is not until the ideas have been evaluated, and perhaps modified to meet the needs of the problem, that "Ideas" are termed "Solutions."

There may be several or many ideas that will be solutions. A basic tenet of the creative process is that there is always more than one right answer. Therefore, some small or partial, easy to implement solutions will emerge, while other more elaborate and important solutions will involve more work to bring into existence. Acknowledging a few of the quick and easy solutions can help problem solvers to regain their equilibrium when faced with difficult problems. Just to realize that some things can be done with little fuss can give encouragement for working out the more complex dimensions of the problem.

The fifth stage of the problem is one that should be "a natural" for librarians. Called *Acceptance Finding*, it is essentially a planning stage. A plan is devised wherein divergent techniques are used to look for all the ways that other persons can be brought in as allies in the process of implementing the solutions to the problem. During this stage problem solvers look objectively at their solutions and see what they need to do to ensure the success of their plan.

Librarians sometimes work out plans without consulting other affected parties, then feel confused and discouraged when their beautiful plan doesn't receive an enthusiastic welcome. If one can't sell a good idea to others, there is something wanting in the plan. Always put yourself in the shoes of the other person and ask, "What's in it for me?" If you can answer that question easily and positively, then you know that you have a plan that is able to gather support from others.

CONCLUSION

The stimulation and nurturing of creativity is a delicate business. Although our complex working environment calls for all of the original and useful ideas we can muster, presented in ways that others can support, sometimes the flow of ideas is impeded by blocks to our creativity from fears or well-ingrained habits. Some of us fear appearing foolish to our peers, we may want to appear confident—to always know the best course of action. Habitual responses can cut short change and growth in ourselves and in others.

Creativity training is not as readily available as some more technologically based training opportunities, but it is worth seeking out. When set in a team-oriented work environment, removed from the hierarchical control systems of earlier generations, creative thinking can help empower library faculty and staff to make the most of their native intelligence, their extensive experience, and their motivation to give good service. While the current times are filled with problems, we are provided with many occasions to constructively use constant change to hone our problem-solving skills to turn problems into challenges, and challenges into opportunities for professional growth.

NOTES

1. Hannelore Rader, telephone conversation with the author, October 7, 1991.

2. Katherine W. Hawkins, "Implementing Team Management in the Modern Library," *Library Administration and Management* 4 (Winter 1989): 11-15.

3. Charles Clarence Williamson, "Melvil Dewey, Creative Librarian," in *Fifty Years of Education for Librarianship* (Urbana: University of Illinois Press, 1943), 3, 5.

4. David Kaser, "Significance, Method, and Creativity in Library Research," in Fiftieth Anniversary, School of Library Science. (Chapel Hill: University of North Carolina at Chapel Hill, 1982), 1-11.

5. William J. J. Gordon, *Synectics: The Development of Creative Capacity* (New York: Harper, 1961).

6. A. J. Anderson, telephone conversation with the author, November 5, 1991.

7. Ibid.

8.   Richard N. Foster, *Innovation: The Attacker's Advantage* (New York: Summit Books, 1986), 28-30.

9.   Magaly Olivero, "Get Crazy: How to Have a Breakthrough Idea," *Working Woman* 15 (September 1990): 144-147.

10.   Amy Saltzman and Edward C. Baig, "Plugging in to 'Creativity'," *U.S. News & World Report* 109 (October 29, 1990): 95-97.

11.   Susan R. Jurow, telephone conversation with the author, December 6, 1991.

12.   Sheila D. Creth, *Effective On-the-Job Training: Developing Library Human Resources* (Chicago: American Library Association, 1986), 6.

13.   Dale E. Shaffer, *A Handbook of Library Ideas* Salem, Ohio: Shaffer, 1977.

14.   Judith Bowen, "Interpersonal and Groupwork Skills," in Handbook of Library Training Practice, ed. Raymond John Prytherch (Brookfield, Vermont: Gower Publishing Company, 1986), 37-60.

15.   Susan R. Jurow, telephone conversation with the author, December 6, 1991.

16.   A. J. Anderson, telephone conversation with the author, November 5, 1991.

17.   A. J. Anderson, *Problems in Library Management* (Littleton, Colorado: Libraries Unlimited, 1981).

18.   *Creative Problem Solving: How to Get Better Ideas.* Videocassette, color, 26 min. (Carlsbad, California: CRM Films, 1979).

19.   Peter Clayton, "Nominal Group Technique and Library Management," *Library Administration and Management* 4 (Winter 1989): 24-26.

20.   Elizabeth Lindsey et al., *Michigan Library Association Workshop Manual* (Lansing, Michigan: Michigan Library Association, 1977), 11, 36.

21.   William J. J. Gordon, *Synectics: The Development of Creative Capacity* (New York: Harper, 1961).

22.   *Training; The Magazine of Human Resources Development* (Minneapolis, Minnesota: Lakewood Publications, Inc., 1964-date).

23.   Ostrye, Anne T., "Creativity in the Workplace," *College and Research Library News* 50 (April 1989): 279-282.

24.   Well-established general training programs in creativity techniques are offered in the United States and other countries by the Creative Education Foundation, 1050 Union Road #4, Buffalo, New York, 14224; The Center for Studies in Creativity, State University of New York, College at Buffalo, 1300 Elmwood Avenue, Buffalo, New York 14222-1095; The Center For Creative Leadership, 5000 Laurinda Drive, Greensboro, North Carolina 27402-1660, Synectics, Inc., 17 Dunster St., Cambridge, Massachusetts 02138, and SES Associates (Synectics Education Systems), 121 Brattle St., Cambridge, Massachusetts 02138.

25.   Sidney J. Parnes, *Creative Thinking Guidebook* (New York: Scribner's, 1967).

26.   Edward deBono, *Lateral Thinking: Creativity Step by Step* (New York: Harper and Row, 1970).

27. John S. Dacey, *Fundamentals of Creative Thinking* (Lexington, Massachusetts: D.C. Heath, 1989).

28. Kaser, 1-11.

29. Alex F. Osborn, *Applied Imagination* (New York: Scribner's, 1963).

30. Parnes.

31. Robert Boice and Ferdinand Jones, "Why Academicians Don't Write," *Journal of Higher Education* 55 (September/October 1984): 568-582.

Chapter 11

PEER TRAINING FOR REFERENCE

Sara B. Sluss

INTRODUCTION

There are many public services librarians, working in libraries with a rapidly increasing number of computer-based services, who visualize the learning curve as follows:

1. Database is ordered/subscribed to/leased.
2. CD-ROM/tape/passwords arrive or are issued.
3. In a setting removed from the reference desk the librarian has an opportunity to examine—without interruption—the database, peruse the manual, prepare instructional guides as needed, and even consult with the vendor regarding anticipated problems or to sign up vendor designed training programs.
4. The database is mounted for public use. Librarians at the reference desk are prepared to answer questions about retrieval software as well as content-based inquiries with confidence.

Welcome to fantasy land. The reality is generally a far cry from this particular vision. The cost of many computer-based services make many librarians blanch and make us disinclined to hold such services back from public use until we are well versed in their intricacies. At costs exceeding thousands of dollars per year, we are reluctant to withhold access for a few weeks or months while the staff (as schedules allow) learns the new service. Additionally, few libraries have the luxury of available back-office workstations equipped either with modems or CD-ROM drives where such uninterrupted study can take place. Manuals are frequently unintelligible, too lengthy, too technical, and seldom address the limits of the database but merely tout its usefulness. Customer assistance from vendors varies from good to nonexistent and training programs (when offered) inexplicably seem to be scheduled at the most inconvenient times and places for your staff. When vendor training is offered, institutional funding to support training is often not available. Few vendors offer on site training programs.

THE NEED FOR PEER TRAINING

It seemed inevitable. At Baruch College we were on a collision course—too much to learn, too little money, everything happening too fast. The library and, consequently, our clients were quickly becoming heavily reliant on an increasing number of technology-based resources. In spite of encouragement by the librarians, students often preferred to wait to use computer-based services while the equivalent or identical source in print form languished in the stacks. Our shrinking materials budget reflected the troubles of both the New York State and entire United States economy. The reduced materials budgets had an impact on the workflow for bibliographers and for acquisitions and cataloging staff and librarians. Bibliographers found that most of their funds were committed to serials and little money was left for selecting monographs. Acquisitions librarians had fewer titles to order. Cataloging librarians had fewer titles to catalog. The money available for staff development was less likely to be forthcoming and, though travel money to conferences was still available, the department's policy was to not process requests for training registration less than fifty dollars, leaving librarians to choose whether or not to pay registration fees for local training out of their own pockets. In the midst of an economic crisis, we continued the planning process for a new state-of-the-art library facility which would be ready to receive us two years hence. The anticipated clash between technology and the library was increasingly reflected in the faces and the demeanor of the librarians.

The mission of the library at Baruch College, one of the senior colleges in the City University of New York, is to prepare our students to be ready to enter the information and service oriented New York City economy. In spite of the faltering fiscal situation, the Baruch Library had a commitment to introduce state-of-the-art services and databases to our students. In 1987 we were a test site for a NOTIS based integrated library system and were working with an OPAC that had grown from the initial 3 test sites to 15 campus libraries. We had invested in approximately thirteen CD-ROM-based databases which were mounted on a local area network. Our students had online access in the library to Dow Jones News Service. The librarians could utilize DIALOG, BRS, OCLC, and RLIN at the reference desk in order to answer reference questions. In just a few years, the library had moved from a card catalog and from a situation where access to all electronic services was mediated by a librarian to a situation where, increasingly, the librarian needed to provide on-the-spot instruction in these services to patrons seated in front of a workstation.

In addition to this shift in how reference questions were answered, there was also a turnover on the professional staff in the library. There had been a 50 percent turnover among those librarians routinely assigned to reference. We also had hired two new catalogers and a serials manager, all of whom had expressed interest in working at the reference desk even though they had little or no experience in reference. But even the "old hands" at reference were still learning all of these new services. All 13 librarians had expressed their concern to me about their lack of knowledge or expertise in one or another of these computer-based services.

As the Associate Librarian for Reader Services I received many flyers from vendors announcing new services, training schedules, and materials. I forwarded the training schedules to my librarians and encouraged attendance. Baruch librarians are fortunate in that many of these vendors are based in New York City and that training opportunities are available locally. Generally, we weren't forced to invest more than a half day's time for any particular training program. But even with that advantage, it was impossible to release more than one or two librarians for training at a time, especially when classes were in session. In addition, we had never resolved the issue of what responsibility the librarian, who has received training at institutional expense, had to return and train her/his colleagues. Allowing librarians to choose among the training opportunities if and when they were offered was not satisfactory. I was also uncomfortable with the concept of assigning a librarian to attend vendor-provided training when I was unable to guarantee funding. And it seemed unreasonable to require a librarian, who had personally paid for the training expense, to come back and train the rest of the professional staff in public services. Teaching one's colleagues in a classroom situation can be anxiety-provoking, and I knew that some of our professional staff would be very reluctant to do so. Short of closing down the reference desk and sending everyone to training courses with a dozen different vendors, I was unsure how to ensure a minimum level of expertise in these services.

SURVEYING STAFF AND ORGANIZING TRAINING

What I was hearing from the librarians was discomfort; there was too much learning on the fly; too much dependence on librarian A as the storehouse of information on database B, on librarian C for database D; and that there was too little time to examine databases away from the firing line that the reference desk had become. I wanted to be sure that what I was hearing was not just the tension that had built up after a two-hour shift at a busy desk, so I determined to systematically survey the attitudes and experiences of all of the librarians who were working at the reference desk. This unscientific survey, with all its faults, is reproduced as the Appendix. I asked the librarians to complete it within a week and return it to me. I specifically asked about their comfort levels as opposed to levels of expertise. At that point I was very concerned for my staff, since all were reporting increasing stress at the reference desk and many indicated that they believed that the stress was the result of the burgeoning number of computer-based services.

The results of the survey were not terribly surprising. Each and every one of the 13 librarians indicated a desire for training in one or more areas. What was remarkable, though, was the outcome on Question # 4: "How 'comfortable' do you feel searching...." I correlated the responses and discovered that for every "Unsure" or "No experience" response, I had someone who felt "Very" comfortable with the service. Further, the responses crossed the lines of seniority and experience. The concept of peer training seemed a perfect match for these circumstances. It allowed for flexibility in scheduling. Those persons indicating that they felt "comfortable" were paired with those who were not and who had indicated they needed more information and/or training. Peer trainers were given the responsibility of contacting their "student(s)," setting up schedules for the training session, preparing any instructional materials that might be used to support the session, and reporting back to me on the session. Peer training allowed each librarian to draw on personal skills and expertise and share them with colleagues in a forum designed to be as unthreatening as possible.

The instructions forwarded to all trainers and trainees stressed that the trainer was not necessarily an expert in this service or database, but had merely expressed a high level of comfort based on experience using the database. I also arranged for several training venues which could be reserved for a block of time: the library's online classroom (both online and CD-ROM access), the office suite for reference librarians (both online and CD-ROM access), and technical services workroom (OCLC access). I asked trainers to not schedule training at the reference desk except before the library opened in the morning. Training sessions were to be kept to under one hour and to be completed, if at all possible, within the following four weeks. Every librarian had at least one training session to prepare and a few had several.

Some trainers developed detailed exercises, others found an informal approach more to their liking. Trainers prepared logon instructions, devised sample questions to search, illustrated examples of problems in searching the database, furnished "cheat sheets" of search keys, and distributed articles discussing search techniques and reviews of databases and services. Some of the trainers arrived at sessions with scribbled notes and others with packets of materials and instructions for their "pupils." In some instances the veterans picked up tips from the novices! Almost everyone was able to complete their training schedule within those four weeks.

EVALUATION AND FUTURE CONSIDERATIONS

Since the survey that started the peer training program was informal, I wanted to keep the follow-up informal, particularly since an evaluation of a one-on-one training could be construed as an evaluation of the person as opposed to the instruction. I relied on verbal feedback of these sessions to provide a sense of their relative success. Comments varied, but most librarians indicated that they found these brief sessions of value. Several librarians expressed an interest in additional sessions.

Perhaps the most interesting and instructional component of this program was the one not anticipated. The peer training sessions arose entirely out of the expressed need for training in specific computer-based services. What had not been designed into this program and had not been anticipated was the improvement in the collegial attitude in the department. When training sessions were assigned, great care was taken to balance the partners. I did not want to reinforce the notion of "haves and have nots" by putting those having expertise at odds with those who have none or little. As a result, not only did everyone have an opportunity to be both pupil and teacher, some leveling took place when junior members found themselves in the position of training senior librarians. The last hired reference librarian trained the library's new training coordinator on a CD-ROM. A new cataloger found herself training an experienced reference librarian on OCLC. The new serials librarian trained an adjunct librarian who worked at the reference desk in keyword searching in CUNY+, our NOTIS based OPAC. A librarian who was generally perceived as "non-technical" was scheduled to train several people in the use of RLIN and developed detailed exercises with sample searches that allowed the trainees to explore RLIN on their own after the session.

Not only did we experience some breakdown in the hierarchy in the unit, but as an extension to planning and presenting these instructional sessions, some formerly resistant librarians began to feel more comfortable about giving small group instruction. A few expressed interest in assisting with course-related lectures and workshops offered by the instructional division of the library.

Another spin-off of this experiment in peer training was a change in the way we now train and utilize clerical staff across divisions in the library. The model by which peering training sessions were employed with the professional staff is now being used to cross-train clerical staff. The reference office assistant trained clerical staff in serials to assist in adding retrospective holdings of reference serials to the OPAC. Circulation staff were trained to work at the Periodicals/Reserve service desk. The impetus for starting cross-training in the clerical units arose from the very pragmatic need to have more than one person with sufficient expertise to run a unit, or to at least keep it functioning at a minimal level, when the regular staff was unavailable due to illness or annual leave.

This is not a flawless plan; there are several caveats. Peer training cannot substitute for vendor-sponsored formal instruction. Although vendor-provided training has limitations, too, the concentrated hands-on training that some vendors offer gives the librarian an opportunity to be totally immersed for a few hours in that particular service. However, the training that the vendors make available cannot supply the secondary benefit of improved collegiality that the peer training sessions did. I believe that peer training will work best in a unit that is not terribly bound by its hierarchy. An informal structure adapts best to this informal training program. A manager who employs peer training must have confidence in the collective abilities of the unit. I was very fortunate to be managing a group of librarians who were flexible, informal, and who brought a wide variety of skills to their work which they were eager to share with their colleagues.

Of course new services become available constantly, and we are planning a repetition and expansion of the peer training exercise in the next phase. In addition to reassessing "comfort" levels with these same services to determine whether growth has occurred and whether further training is desired, we also have access to, or will be acquiring, services for which training will be necessary. We will add to the next survey questions about the Internet, FTP, First Search, Census CD-ROMs, text CD-ROMs such as WordCruncher, and searching the Wilson databases which were recently added to CUNY+. This is not fantasy land, but peer training can help reference librarians deal with the realities of contemporary reference services.

APPENDIX

1. Have you attended general DIALOG training in the last five years?
2. Have you attended training on any specific DIALOG database or family of databases (i.e., Predicasts) in the last five years?
    If yes, please list database(s).
3. Did you attend EPIC training?
4. How "comfortable" do you feel searching the following? (5 = Very Comfortable, 3 = OK, 1 = Unsure, 0 = No experience)

RLIN	5	4	3	2	1	0
CLC	5	4	3	2	1	0
DIALOG, generally	5	4	3	2	1	0
DJNS	5	4	3	2	1	0
CD-ROMS, generally[1]	5	4	3	2	1	0
CUNY+ keyword[2]	5	4	3	2	1	0
LEXIS/NEXIS[3]	5	4	3	2	1	0

5. For which of the following would you be interested in receiving more training? Circle all that apply.
    RLIN
    OCLC
    DIALOG
    DJNS
    CUNY+ keyword

LEXIS/NEXIS

CD-ROMS (specify which)

6. Are the library's policies for ready reference online searching (specifically in DIALOG databases) clear to you?

7. Would you be interested in doing more online (i.e., DIALOG, LEXIS/NEXIS) searching, and specifically, more complex searches? Do you have any interest in being trained to provide back-up for Baruch's online search services? [4]

NOTES

1. In retrospect I realized that it would have been much more helpful to determine exactly which CD-ROMS each librarian was comfortable with and for which training was desired. If I were to repeat this survey, I would revise it to cluster UMI CD-ROMs (e.g., ABI Inform Ondisc, Newspaper Abstracts Ondisc, Dissertation Abstracts Ondisc), SilverPlatter CD-ROMs (e.g., PAIS, PsycLit, Sociofile), and list separately those with unique searching software (e.g., National Trade Data Bank, World Currency Monitor, Compact D/SEC, Econ/Stats).

2. CUNY+ is our NOTIS-based OPAC.

3. The library had been using LEXIS/NEXIS exclusively in a mediated searching mode, but we were anticipating a change in procedure with Mead's announcement of a new fee structure for academic business libraries. Even though most librarians indicated a desire for LEXIS/NEXIS training, we postponed scheduling. Mead now offers their own training sessions at no charge, frequently repeated, and tailored for various levels of expertise.

4. We had one librarian in charge of mediated online searching and I hoped to be able to identify, by way of this survey, one or more librarians who would be interested in providing back-up assistance. At the time of this survey we had not yet seen the impact that the increasing availability of CD-ROMs would have on mediated searching requests.

Chapter 12

STAFF DEVELOPMENT AND MENTORING

Lynn K. Milet

INTRODUCTION

Staff is the most important resource we have in libraries. The staff shapes the library's image by providing library services and by being the first and often the primary contact between the user and library services.[1]

The decade of the 1990s has brought with it a number of major challenges to libraries. Rapidly changing information technologies are causing what might be called "techno-stress" among library staff. Library administrators need to be responsive to the change process and provide staff with the skills they need to cope with the new environments associated with technological change. New procedures, new policies, new staff patterns, and changing user needs all occur as information technologies change. Staff cannot be expected to make the transition to a new working environment, with new responsibilities, without some apprehension and frustration coupled with a steep learning curve.

Libraries are also challenged by sociological changes. A more diverse, multicultural user base needs different approaches to services; while a more diverse, multicultural library staff requires new approaches to staff training and job responsibilities.

Economic challenges are forcing library administrators to consider alternate administrative and organizational approaches that are more flexible and adaptable to the challenges we face than the more traditional ones. Some relevant trends that are developing include making maximum use of staff by creating multifunctional teams, emphasizing processes rather than procedures, decentralization of some activities, reallocating resources, and making staff leaner and flatter.[2]

These challenges and changes will require that staff be more adaptable, willing and able to assume new and more responsibilities, and better able to work with other people in a team atmosphere.

Mentoring today implies a one-to-one nurturing relationship between a senior level or supervisory staff member and a junior level or subordinate staff member. We consider mentors as counselors who give advice, and sponsors who share contacts and use their influence to enhance the career development of their protégés. These relationships require a long-term commitment on the part of both parties to spend significant amounts of time and energy in developing and maintaining the relationship.[3]

In professional development areas, mentors give their protégés advice on what their goals should be and how to achieve them. If the career path is within the library, the mentor assists the protégé in determining what programs and educational opportunities would help them best in their current position as well as in advancing within the library organization.

If the career path is outside of the library, the mentor assists the staff member in determining what his or her goals are for promotional opportunities elsewhere and how best to achieve those goals.

In both cases the mentor provides the necessary evaluation and feedback of the protégé's activities to help him or her build strengths and improve weaknesses. All this should occur in a trusting and nurturing environment.

The mentor can also play a psychosocial role if the protégé so desires, by honing skills for planning lifetime goals, self-confidence, personal behavior, and teaching the protégé how to achieve short and long term personal objectives.

Developing a mentor program is an often difficult task. Some organizations develop formal programs that involve pairing a senior staff member with a junior staff member. The main purpose of these programs is to introduce and/or indoctrinate a new or newly promoted employee with organizational goals in relation to their work responsibilities. Although these programs can serve an important function, there are problems.[4]

Formalization of the process tends to reduce the trust or intimacy between a mentor and protégé when that relationship is "forced" rather than allowed to develop naturally and gradually over time.

Formal programs often pair supervisors with junior staff. If the protégé is a subordinate of the mentoring supervisor, that relationship can lead to the perception of favoritism by other staff working for the same supervisor. If the mentoring supervisor is not the protégé's supervisor, the protégé may feel a conflict between what his or her supervisor says and the advice of the mentor.

Informal mentoring involves the spontaneous development of a relationship between the mentor and protégé. Although this is a more natural way to encourage mentoring, there is very little control over the process. The possibility exists that some junior staff who would benefit the most from a mentoring relationship would not find such a relationship or that an employee might choose the wrong mentor or protégé and become frustrated and disillusioned by the process.[5]

Other relationships deserve our attention as well when considering the mentoring process. Although senior and supervisory staff are the most frequent people to act as mentors, colleagues and peers can also be effective in the role. They can serve as sounding boards for ideas as well as help solve problems.

We need to encourage and develop open channels of communication and shared expectations. All this requires an emphasis on mentoring, continuing education, training, and programs that allow for personal growth.

THE LEHIGH EXPERIENCE

The Lehigh University Library System, with an operating budget for 1991-92 of $2.5 million, consists of three libraries, which house 1,005,000 volumes, 4,800 serial subscriptions, 503,000 government documents, and 28,000 non-print media units. The library staff includes 21 FTE professional staff, and 47 FTE non-professional (support) staff, FTE. We have 4,489 undergraduate students, 2,076 graduate students, 411 full-time faculty, 85 adjuncts and visiting scholars/researchers and 1,000 staff.

The Lehigh University library had always been responsive to staff development needs, and in 1989 the library administration made a formal commitment to staff development. At that time the Director of Libraries created a Mentoring and Training Task Force with a charge to design a formal staff development program that would provide both professional and support staff with work-related and personal growth activities. The Task Force includes four professional staff, three support staff, and three "ex- officio" members who are called in as consultants on an as-needed basis. The original members were appointed for either two or three year terms, so that we can rotate membership and maintain a "fresh approach" to our charge. As the Task Force Chair, I am the one permanent member of the committee.

One of our first assignments was to research and read material concerning staff development and mentoring in order to better understand our objectives. The Task Force meets at least three times a year, at the beginning of each semester and at the end of the Spring semester, to decide on programs and assign responsibilities.

Over the past three years the Task Force has developed a very effective and popular program that includes educational and training programs to enhance knowledge and understanding of work-related issues; programs that seek to change behavior in the workplace; programs dealing with personal needs and behaviors leading to self-actualization and increased self-awareness; and an informal mentoring program. Staff development programs include formal workshops, in-service days, guest speakers, and informal social activities. All of these support our informal mentoring program. The Task Force sponsors two activities each academic semester, and two during the summer.

Most of the programs we offer are general enough in nature to include both professional and support staff participation; but there are some programs that are directed toward specific staff populations.

Programs are evaluated by participants and workshop facilitators and the results are shared with both the Task Force and the full library staff. Staff are continually asked for input and suggestions for future programs.

WORKSHOPS

The workshops we offer cover a variety of work-related topics. We have offered half-day workshops, facilitated by both professional and support staff, on specific computer software applications that are used in the Library. For example, workshops in WordPerfect, QuattroPro, and dBase have been given because these are the programs the staff must use for word processing, database management, and statistical analysis. Sessions are offered for first time users as well as advanced users. The Lehigh Libraries use the GEAC online system, so our staff have presented "short courses" in new GEAC subsystems as well as review sessions of subsystems already in use. To reinforce newly acquired skills, library staff (both support and professional, who are proficient in a particular program, volunteer to act as "troubleshooters" for staff who are not as familiar with a system. After taking one of the workshops, a participant is "assigned" a staff member whom they can call if they experience a problem while using a computer program or GEAC subsystem.

Our reference staff offers monthly one-hour sessions on issues related to reference, but any interested staff member is encouraged to attend. Examples of these sessions include a hands-on demonstration of our CD-ROM local area networks, and a demonstration of online databases we are able to access through the Internet.

Other workshops offered by library staff include one on HyperCard library applications, a session for supervisors on how to mentor, and a workshop to train one person in each area to troubleshoot the microcomputers and CD-ROM stations we use.

The Pennsylvania Area Library Network (PALINET) offers workshops on many library-related issues and computer software programs. Their workshop schedule is distributed on a regular basis to the professional staff who are encouraged to register themselves or send a support staff member if it is appropriate. The library pays all costs for the trip to Philadelphia (an hour's ride from Lehigh), where workshops are held.

SUPPORT STAFF IN-SERVICE DAYS

Each year the library holds a support staff in-service day. The day starts at 8 a.m. with a 30 minute coffee and doughnut kick-off. Three 90 minute sessions are held during the day, providing staff with ample opportunity to attend all three workshops. The sessions are offered twice in the morning with a 15 minute break in between and one in the afternoon. Participants are treated by the library to a 90 minute lunch. At 3 p.m. participants gather for refreshments to relax for a while and discuss what they have learned. The day ends at 3:30 p.m.

This program started because, unlike professional staff who have opportunities to attend professional conferences, support staff are confined by their daily routines. A special in-service day for support staff gives these employees an opportunity to learn about other departments and activities in the library. It also gives them time to spend with peers they rarely interact with, because of their diverse work locations.

PROFESSIONAL DEVELOPMENT

Employees need to view their role within the library, define their work, and gain professional recognition. To this end all professional staff are encouraged to attend and participate in professional meetings; locally, statewide, and nationally.

Lehigh believes all staff should be able to take advantage of educational opportunities, whether it involves work-related information, or something of personal interest to the staff member. All staff, professional and support, are encouraged to take courses through the tuition remission benefit offered by Lehigh to full-time employees. Every effort is made to accommodate staff who need to take time off during the work-day to attend classes, a workshop, or a conference. Many of our staff have taken advantage of this benefit and have received B.S., M.S., M.Ed., Ed.D., and Ph.D degrees while working full-time in the library.

Lehigh is a member of the Patriot League Consortium of Libraries, made up of Lehigh, Bucknell, U. S. Military Academy at West Point, Colgate, Fordham, College of Holy Cross, Lafayette, and the U.S. Naval Academy at Annapolis. A special consortium exchange program provides librarians with the opportunity to exchange jobs for a period of time within the consortium libraries. This provides another way in which they can learn about their profession as well as themselves.

SOCIAL EVENTS

The Mentoring and Training Task Force provides opportunities for all staff to get together in an informal atmosphere to share ideas. Trips to other libraries, including a day trip to Washington, D.C. to tour the Library of Congress, brown-bag lunch movies or guest speakers, and late afternoon teas all provide a relaxed setting where the staff can share experiences and learn about each other.

LIBRARY-RELATED COMMITTEES

To encourage team work, the majority of library committees include both professional and support staff members. Although most committees are chaired by professional staff, there are some committees that are often chaired by support staff. This opportunity to work side-by-side helps eliminate the we-they syndrome, create a cooperative atmosphere in which everyone has worth, and foster and develop leadership skills.

BEHAVIOR MODIFICATION

Education and training has traditionally been what people think of when they define staff development. Our Task Force, like many organizations, realized the challenges facing libraries and library staff would require a staff development program that included more than education and training. Staff need to understand themselves in order to deal with the changes facing them now and in the future. Thus, we also offer programs that are meant to help change behavior that is both work related and personal.

We have, with the help of the Lehigh University Office of Human Resources, offered half-day workshops in time management skills, stress management, Meyers Briggs Personality Assessment, crisis management, first aid, CPR, making effective presentations, and diversity (multicultural) training.

One of the first workshops we ever offered, and probably one of the most important to our total program, was a workshop offered to supervisors and managers on how to mentor and respond to staff needs and requests. Nothing can be more frustrating to an employee than knowing the library policy is to encourage staff development, but having a supervisor who will not approve the time off.

Some of these workshops require hiring facilitators from outside the University, which results in a workshop fee. The library and the Human Resources department usually share in the costs. These workshops are popular and help staff deal with many work-related changes.

PERSONAL SKILLS OR GROWTH PROGRAMS

Productive employees are ones who can deal effectively with problems and issues in their personal lives. The Mentoring and Training Task Force recognizes this fact and offers programs meant to help staff deal with personal problems. Examples of programs we have offered are: a session dealing with health benefits—the difference between our options, how to send in insurance forms, and what we are entitled to; a session concerning education benefits—what they are, who in a family is entitled to them, and how to take advantage of them; a session on single parenting—how to deal with work, home, and family; and a session concerning working full-time and going to school—how to juggle responsibilities and focus on the task at hand. Some of us act as mentors, available to listen to a problem or give advice on an issue we have experience with; such as being a single parent, working full-time and going to school, or dealing with a difficult student or faculty client.

MENTORING

Rather than develop a formal mentoring program, the Task Force wanted to create an atmosphere in which informal relationships would develop and be fostered. All the programs described in this chapter are designed to bring staff together in different environments to get to know each other and to develop mentoring relationships. Since there is little control over what happens, all staff are aware of our efforts and are encouraged to work with someone if they feel that person needs help in some area. Because of this informal program, we currently have a number of mentoring relationships between professional and professional, professional and support, and support and support staff. Some mentors are supervisors or senior staff members and some are colleagues or peers of their protégés. These relationships are based on both professional and personal needs and all seem to be flourishing.

RECOMMENDATIONS

1. Develop a program to encourage mentoring relationships.
2. Form a committee to deal with staff development issues rather than making it the responsibility of one person. Make sure the committee has a diverse membership.
3. Provide a variety of programs and do not focus only on issues or concerns related to the work environment.
4. Make sure the library administration supports these efforts and allows the time for workshops, in-service days, and so forth.
5. Work with supervisors and managers to teach them how to mentor and respond to staff requests. Staff development requires flexibility which is more difficult for some of us than others.

6. Build in an evaluation component for all activities and allow all staff to input their suggestions for future programs.

CONCLUSION

The Lehigh Library administration, through the Mentoring and Training Task Force, has worked hard to develop an eclectic staff development program that meets the needs of a diverse employee group. It has been well worth the time and effort. We will continue to make modifications to existing programs and add new programs in an effort to support staff as the library environment and staff expectations continue to change.

NOTES

1. Anne Lipow, "Training for Change: Staff Development in a New Age," *Journal of Library Administration* 10 (1989): 87-97.
2. Colin Coulson-Thomas, "Developing Tomorrow's Professionals Today," *Journal of European Industrial Training* 15, no. 1 (1991): 3-11.
3. Beverly Harris-Schenz, " Helping With The Bootstraps: The Mentor's Task," *ADFL Bulletin* 21, no. 3 (1990): 18-21.
4. Maria Shelton, "Mentoring: Bridge Over Troubled Water," *Journal of School Leadership* 1 (1991): 38-44.
5. Linda Johnsrud, "Mentor Relationships: Those That Help and Those That Hinder," *New Directions for Higher Education* 18, no. 4 (1990): 57-66.

REFERENCE

Shaughnessy, Thomas "Staff Development in Libraries: Why It Frequently Doesn't Take." *Journal of Library Administration* 9, no. 2 (1988): 5-12.

Chapter 13

THE EVERGREEN STATE COLLEGE: PROFESSORS AT THE REFERENCE DESK

Taylor E. Hubbard

INTRODUCTION

The quotable pundit once observed that every picture is an answer to the question, "What is Art?" Something similar might be said of the faculty/librarian rotation plan at The Evergreen State College: each rotation adds new definition to the experience. Evergreen is one of the campuses under the state of Washington's system of higher education. Since 1980, ten years after the founding of this non-traditional liberal arts college, faculty and librarians have regularly been exchanging places between the classroom and the reference desk. This program has become one of the many distinctive and lasting features of a college well known for adopting the unusual in pursuit of the excellent.

Teaching is at the core of Evergreen's educational philosophy. Obvious as this may seem for any educational institution, at Evergreen the spokes which radiate from the teaching hub include a variety of learning strategies such as undergraduate seminars, internships, and individual learning contracts. Faculty librarians are committed to the concept of a teaching library, putting into practice at the reference desk and in the classroom teaching/ learning modes and strategies common to the general curriculum.

In practical terms, this means that bibliographic instruction becomes an integrated part of the academic offerings of the college, and faculty librarians assume the responsibility of designing library research elements which are coordinated into the subject matter of the course offerings.

The rotation scheme is made possible in part by the non-traditional nature of the curriculum and structure of the college. The fullest description of Evergreen's philosophy, programs and methods was written by Richard Jones in 1981.[1] Despite its advancing age, Jones' book remains the most cogent overview of the college, and of its instruction methods and expectations. One important feature is that most programs (known elsewhere as courses) are interdisciplinary in content and team taught by two to four faculty from different disciplines. For this reason, faculty have been recruited because of their interest in collaborative teaching. Program content is developed by the team, and will normally constitute a student's entire course load for the duration of the program, usually two to three quarters. Evergreen has no academic departments for its 175 faculty. Instead there are several "specialty areas" which function as discussion and planning groups for various disciplines; Political Economy and Social Change, for example, is a forum for a broad range of social scientists, although membership is open to anyone, regardless of discipline. Librarians join any of these interest groups. The absence of departmental turf contributes to the collaborative, interdisciplinary character of the curriculum. Similarly, there are no academic ranks among faculty; salaries are determined solely by years of experience with the result that academic status-related tensions and competitions familiar to some readers tend to be absent from campus discourse at Evergreen. The absence of traditional academic structures plus innovative course design have been major contributors to the facility with which the library and librarians interact with academic colleagues.

Devising an instructional program based on critical approaches to information has established the library as an integral part of the campus teaching community, and has also established librarians as full members of the faculty with the same hiring process, same contracts, same campus responsibilities, same salary scales, and same academic standing. The six reference faculty are organized as a team parallel to other campus instructional programs with a rotating chairperson (in Evergreen parlance, "convener") chosen from year to year. The reference convener sits on an advisory group with other conveners who, along with the curriculum dean, coordinate the instructional programs of the general curriculum. Personnel management responsibilities which elsewhere would be the responsibility of a head of reference are shared among reference faculty, leaving to the convener budget management and most of the unit's administrative details, shared with an administrative assistant. All library decisions are made by a formalized consensus process adopted in recent years. Collection development is shared among reference faculty and members of the staff of the library.

The somewhat unique equality of academic librarians and faculty at Evergreen provides the foundation for the faculty/ librarian rotation plan which has been in effect since librarians were granted full faculty status in 1980. Prior to this, beginning in 1978, faculty could request assignment to the library for one quarter, without comparable librarian rotation.

To understand how faculty become available for library assignment, it is useful to know something of the structure of the curriculum at the college. The annual program offerings of the college leave some faculty unassigned. This unassigned group includes those on leave, sabbatical, exchanges, or those available for teaching stand alone courses, sponsoring individual contracts, or similar instructional assignments including rotation to the library. The reference faculty reviews the pool of unassigned faculty and invites one or more faculty to join them during the year. The number of rotating faculty will be same as the number of librarians scheduled to teach in the academic programs that year. Until 1992, faculty librarians taught outside the library one out of every nine quarters. For at least the next two years, beginning in fall of 1992, some rotations will be for two quarters as a result of a teaching faculty member being selected as Dean of Library Services.

Fairly specific guidelines were developed for rotating faculty by reference faculty in 1985. Although this document is somewhat formal in its delineation of responsibilities, in Evergreen's ever-evolving practice there is a certain elasticity in interpretation, which accommodates the informalities of an academic community not enthusiastic about creating or adhering to entangling rules and regulation. In summary the current specifics for rotating faculty are:

1. As a primary responsibility, serve at the Reference Desk as scheduled and complete collection development projects in a designated subject area.
2. Work closely with one librarian who will serve as mentor.
3. Participate in library governance groups and work with the Resource Selection Committee which oversees the materials budget and major purchases.
4. Adhere to standard library practices regarding interaction with users, confidentiality of records, and similar library conventions.
5. Write an evaluation of the library experience, equivalent to the program evaluation written by faculty teaching in the general curriculum.

These expectations are agreed upon prior to the rotation assignment. The assignment begins on the first day of the quarter. About half of the rotations occur during the fall quarter when one of the faculty librarians is teaching in the general curriculum. The remainder are about evenly divided between winter and spring quarters. The majority of rotations are for only one quarter, although there have been at least three two-quarter assignments.

"Training" suggests a far more formal process than is in fact the practice for a faculty member joining the reference team; "orientation" is probably the more accurate description. Faculty members will have differing levels of expectations and expertise. Experience has shown that there is a strong correlation between being an accomplished library user and being a rotating faculty. For example, some faculty who have rotated to the reference desk, are also frequent users of the shelflist, esoteric indexes and the *National Union Catalog*. Therefore, rotation for some is preaching to the choir. Nonetheless, becoming practiced in the way other disciplines organize and use research and information is a uniformly new experience for most.

It is the mentor who assumes much of the responsibility for organizing the faculty member's time and experience. Any of the reference librarians can act as mentor. It is usually considerations of subject interest, availability, friendships or workloads which figure in the assignment. The mentor is primarily responsible for making sure all the experiential bases have been covered during the period of the rotation. The mentor is only the ultimate resource person for the faculty member; all reference librarians provide orientation in their own particular areas of interest and expertise, and are informal resource persons whenever the need or occasion arises. This most frequently happens when one of the reference faculty shares desk duty with the faculty member.

The primer for reference work is the in-house text prepared for a library research course irregularly offered by the reference faculty.[2] The booklet covers the research process, documentation, presenting research and a bibliography of basic reference sources in academic subject areas. Since it is geared to features of this library, it constitutes a crash course for reference desk duty by supplying answers to many of the locational and facilities questions which come over the reference desk, as well as providing highlights of the Evergreen reference collection.

Reference desk assignment is a priority in the rotation, usually at least 12-15 hours per week. During the ten weeks of a quarter, faculty seldom become proficient enough to be alone at the desk, so they usually work in tandem with more experienced reference faculty. Desk shifts are usually for two to three hours. From the beginning, faculty are encouraged to field as many questions as they feel comfortable with. This is a number which grows substantially over the quarter, in part because many questions are related to library use such as PAC operation, holdings, locations, completing interlibrary loan forms and verification, and operating various compact disc services in the reference area.

Subject reference is, by consensus, the most challenging part of the rotations for faculty. For a small liberal arts college (3200 students), the reference collection has remarkable depth in most subject areas with the exceptions of technology and business.

Indexing services in the collection include all the citation indexes, many of the Commonwealth Agricultural indexes, all U.S. government indexes, including NTIS, basic indexes in areas of the humanities, particularly in film, philosophy, religion and literature; and all major social sciences indexes, with subfields in public affairs, geography, anthropology, psychology and sociology. To these are added the growing number of indexes for minority and gender issues, and substantial depth in resources for environmental studies, public administration and education which have small graduate programs at the college. Many of these are being replaced by electronic versions, either in compact disc form or, as with *Biological Abstracts* and *Chemical Abstracts*, by more universally accessible online access. There is also a working collection for case and statutory law.

The quantity of reference literature, and the interdisciplinary nature of the programs at Evergreen mean that becoming acquainted with this collection is virtually the full-time preoccupation of newly arrived faculty. Not only must the bibliography of subject areas be learned, but links must also be made between them to satisfy the interdisciplinary nature of the curriculum offerings. Thinking interdisciplinarily about the interrelationship of subjects means that a wide perspective must be used when responding to research questions. As a consequence, research needs which might under other circumstance be met by using one source, in the Evergreen context may lead to investigating many sources. Moreover, the instructional role of faculty librarians is taken quite seriously: not only are students supplied with answers, but also with lessons on how subjects can be interrelated across disciplines and how the literature of those disciplines is organized. As a consequence, reference desk work is more than simply finding the answer.

Almost without exception, rotating faculty have been very sensitive about the limits of their knowledge of reference works. They have been straightforward in seeking assurance and reassurance that the answers they are supplying, or information they are finding, is both appropriate and the best available in the collection. Intricate questions are often team-researched with the experienced person scheduled with the faculty. As the faculty become more secure in fielding reference questions, usually mid-way through the quarter, they are able to handle much of the reference traffic alone, albeit with a librarian as backup.

The bibliographic instruction program developed by the library faculty is incorporated into faculty training, and faculty are encouraged to help design and participate in those activities. Initially, this may only amount to observing classes. With more experience, faculty participate in classes—explaining indexes, doing sample searches and the like. Classes may vary in content from workshops for skills related to using citation indexes and learning Boolean searching strategies, to critical and analytic approaches to research literature, using interdisciplinary or multicultural approaches to any topic under study by an academic program. As many faculty self-evaluations maintain, becoming aware of ways that traditional reference sources can be exploited and incorporated into programs is sometimes the greatest benefit of the rotation scheme. And, because reference bibliography can provide particularly striking examples of how disciplines establish knowledge, faculty often leave the library with deeper awareness of the socially constituted character of information and its organization, learned as part of the critical approach to reference taken by reference faculty.

By mid-quarter, five weeks into the rotation, the kinds of research assignments being made by campus programs is well known; the faculty member has had an opportunity to observe or participate in the instruction other librarians are doing for programs; and something of a research ambiance for the quarter has settled in, leaving more time for projects or investigating some of the secondary reference works. Despite the routine and the increasing reference accomplishments which are acquired and developed over the one quarter rotation, faculty are not scheduled for evening or weekend desk hours. As a result, the reference faculty's strength becomes diluted, as or because they are covering for one member teaching in the general curriculum, and working with a replacement whose experience level makes the exchange somewhat uneven in the day-to-day work of reference.

During the rotation, faculty have not given up their non-teaching responsibilities. These include substantial amounts of campus committee work, consulting, individual contracts and conference-going which are faculty librarian responsibilities, as well. To general obligations, the library itself contributes upwards of four or five hours a week of meetings for reference faculty, resource selection, and personnel matters, all of which the rotating faculty member is expected to attend and contribute. For example, the most recent faculty member to join the library chaired the selection committee for identifying a new library dean.

As of Spring of 1992, twenty-three faculty have participated in the rotation plan. This is roughly 12.5% of the current faculty. Nearly half of these have been from the humanities-arts areas. Since the library also includes an ambitious media services program with rotating faculty of its own, not all rotations have been to the reference desk—at least two have been to the Media Center. By discipline, humanities-arts, particularly faculty in fine arts, have been a majority of faculty involved in rotation. This is exactly twice the number of faculty from natural sciences (five). Social sciences falls between the two with seven faculty. In the three disciplinary divisions used by the college catalog, 20% of the humanities-arts faculty have participated in the rotation; about 10% of the social sciences faculty, and 12% of the natural sciences faculty. From the total group there is a high number of faculty from non-bibliographic disciplines—dance, film, physics, architecture. There is one unifying factor among all these faculty, however. With one earlier exception, all faculty who have participated in the rotation were appointed to the college in the ten years between 1970 and 1979; the mean year of appointment is 1972, the year the college officially opened for full time instruction. Until fall of 1986, only male faculty participated in the rotation program. Since that time the majority (six) has been composed of women.

There are a number of possibilities which may explain the predominance of senior faculty in the rotation program. One is that senior faculty may perceive the library as more germane to their instructional goals than newer faculty; older faculty see the library as less alien to their own or curriculum interest and have had long experience with librarians as colleagues since some library faculty are, in seniority, peers of the self-proclaimed "dinosaurs." The dinosaurs are a relatively small group, bonded by the experience of establishing the college's programs over 20 years ago. It is also this generation of faculty which reviewed and approved the rotation plan as well as faculty status for librarians, so they are fully aware of the significance of the program. Newer faculty may be more intent on immersing themselves in the Evergreen experience and developing team teaching techniques by working with more experienced faculty. Consolidating teaching experience is strongly encouraged by the college, so it is not until faculty reach more experienced levels that they may feel available for rotation. Also many new faculty go immediately into programs which tend to be full time commitments for an entire academic year.

There is general consensus that the rotation plan, now entering its fifteenth year, is a great success. It has provided powerful evidence of the importance of the library as an integral part of Evergreen's curriculum. However, as many evaluations maintain, there is a strong case for extending the rotation period. In the three instances when this has been possible, participants have been unanimous in thinking that the minimum rotation should be for two quarters. The one consistent experience of faculty rotating into the library is that one quarter is only sufficient for orienting her/ him to the reference desk, and becoming proficient with only the more routine aspect of reference service. By the time proficiency reaches the level of confidence which allows the faculty member some independence in applying what he/she has learned, the quarter is finished. The few two-quarter experiences have been encouragingly successful. The additional quarter gave the faculty time to become more fluent in providing reference service and apply much of the first quarter's learning. This translated into time to design and/or teach bibliographic instruction units and to make far more valuable contributions to the materials selection process.

Experience has also shown that the second quarter provides the faculty with a valuable voice to participate as a library insider and peer of the staff. In the most recent rotation, in the second quarter the faculty member was able to assume one of the weekend slots on his own, and served alone at the reference desk at other times. This relieved some of the pressure created when an experienced librarian was absent and teaching in the general curriculum. In this case, the second quarter also created enough time to learn the basics of online (DIALOG) searching, a service that is an increasingly important reference service in this library. Online searching has begun (and is expected to continue) to replace print index subscriptions; consequently, library policy has been to provide these services without charge to students as well as faculty. Another faculty member in the library for two quarters was able to contribute enormously to the group investigating the future and expansion of computer services on campus. Because of his experience as a surrogate reference person, his perceptions about the library and librarians' role in the direction that computerization of campus might take meant that the groups recommendations take full advantage of the instructional and information-finding expertise which the library faculty has developed. These kinds of unexpected benefits are a norm with the rotation program.

Whatever the duration of the stay at the reference desk, faculty do appear to go back to teaching with a strong sense of their own ability to incorporate Bibliographic Instruction (BI) into program content. As a result, librarians find a predisposition toward BI when they approach teaching teams, and more frequently find a demand for integrated library experience for classes. Moreover, because of class size (20 students per faculty), team taught courses with four faculty have 80 students and can be an overwhelming size for one librarian to work with effectively. Having one or more faculty team members fluent in research techniques and tools is a bit like having a pool of extra librarians to draw from.

AN EVALUATION EPILOGUE

Annual reviews at Evergreen are focused on each faculty member's self-evaluation. This document is meant to be a thoughtful review of the year's activities and undertakings. The self-evaluation is shared with others—program team members or, in the case of the library faculty, among the reference team—who make written response to it. Any teaching faculty, including librarians, also write evaluations of students, and receive evaluations in return. Because there are no grades for Evergreen programs, written evaluations become the record of student achievement and the substance of all student transcripts. For the faculty member, including librarians, these documents become part of a permanent 'portfolio' maintained by each faculty member as part of the personnel record. Following are some examples from library files of evaluations faculty have made of their rotation experience. One writes:

I promised last spring when I left the library that I would provide you with a more detailed assessment of my experience. While I only worked in the library half-time and was thus not able to do anywhere near as much as I would have liked, what I was able to do seems to me to have been a tremendous value to my teaching and I hope to the library as well. Working on the reference desk was a fun and revealing experience. It was exciting to see the incredibly broad range of questions and problems which the reference librarian is called upon to answer simply because he is sitting behind a desk with an "Ask Me" sign on it. From townspeople I received questions ranging from the location of restrooms to the latest data gathered by the RUDAT research. But I was most impressed by the kinds of questions ranging from mass spectroscopy to Hindu symbolism; from the production of rice in China (literally) to the natural history of desert spiders. The challenge of learning to use the available references, of learning how to use the library better for my own uses, and learning how to use reference in a way that will help my students better use the library was a fun one to meet.

The chance to review the library's holdings in light of major bibliographies in political science and environmental studies provided me with an understanding of the strengths and weaknesses of the library's collections. In both cases it appeared to me that while the collection is adequate (political science) or minimally adequate (environmental studies), significant strengthening of the actual collection (as opposed to the reference collection) will be necessary if we are to undertake graduate effort in these or related fields. In general I was impressed with the need for the college to continually emphasize strengthening its collections in order to meet the extremely varied needs of programs. I realize that it must at times appear tempting to cut acquisitions, but that approach would be a false economy in terms of providing a quality education. It is discouraging to locate just the right article or book to start a project only to find that it has to be acquired on interlibrary loan and won't be available for a week or two.

Another advantage to me in working in the library was the extent I was able to pursue my interests in assembling bibliography and materials for my work this year in the Comparative Environmental Studies program.

On those slow Thursday afternoons (there were some), I often spent two
or three hours developing bibliography from the Environment Index or
the Environmental Periodicals Index. I was able to create a massive pile
of summer reading in Environmental Economics and have used much of
what I learned in my lectures this fall. Finally, this fall, when I wanted
to get my advanced students to work on a major library research project,
I was able to work with [one of the reference faculty] in developing a much
more extensive and grandiose library tour than I would have felt
comfortable asking him to provide on his own. I was comfortable spending
six hours teaching students in the library the complexities and excitement
of bibliographic research. It has definitely paid off in the quality of their
work thus far.

I don't mean this to sound totally ecstatic, I could have used more
guidance and help in the selection process, but without doubt this was the
single most important piece of faculty development work I have done since
I started working here seven years ago. I feel most every faculty member
could benefit from the experience.

Another faculty member felt the rotation experience significant
enough to address a memo to all faculty:

This quarter I had the good fortune to work in our library as part of this
year's faculty library exchange. This annual opportunity allows a member
of the faculty to work full time in the library for one quarter free from
formal teaching responsibilities while one of the librarians rotates into full
time teaching.

I worked as an apprentice reference librarian for part of each week. I
served on active duty at the reference desk which was a sometimes
exhausting though always stimulating contact with students, staff, faculty
and community patrons. I familiarized myself with our library collection
in the specific curriculum area of environmental design with the express
goal of developing resource selection requests in the design related fields
of architecture, planning, ecology and behavior.

This work was an excellent interdisciplinary experience in professional
development. I came in close contact with professional librarians with
training in environmental and social science, art and humanities, law and
government documents. It was an outstanding opportunity to refresh my
knowledge of current library research techniques, reference tools and the
recent literature in environmental design. I developed a working knowledge
of our excellent human library resources and facilities.

As a detailed and comprehensive introduction to library research tools
I highly recommend the Library Evening Course [*Library Research
Methods*] which enables you "to find information about virtually every
subject." I came in working contact with the reality that Evergreen's library

has among the highest rates of circulation per student of any in the State's four year public college systems, some 30 books circulated per student during 1976-77.

The importance of the faculty library exchange is that active working contact is established between two essential elements of our institution, the library and the faculty. The primary aims of the exchange are effective library utilization and active collection development linked to current and future curricular needs. A simultaneous benefit is the personal professional development of library and faculty participants.

My main recommendation is to extend the faculty library exchange period. One quarter is too short. It is currently a good beginning for the development of a working knowledge of library tools and collection building. Two quarters would provide a more effective opportunity for professional development and performance. Let me close with an exhortation for continued and growing faculty and library contact and collaboration.

And yet another faculty member writes:

...Through all this I have learned about a different side of Evergreen. I have learned to value the teaching that goes on in the library and I will change the way I use both the library and the staff with my students from now on. I know who does what, what faculty use the library, what they expect librarians to do for them, what is reasonable to expect them to do, what works and what doesn't work. This exchange has been invaluable for this reason alone. For, while I did make use of the library myself and in my teaching before this experience, I was not efficient and I had a rather single minded view of what should be done. That has all changed.

NOTES

1. Richard M. Jones, *Experiment at Evergreen* (Cambridge, MA: Schenkman Books, Inc., 1981).

2. Pat Matheny-White and Barbara Bergquist, *Library Research Methods* (Olympia, WA: The Evergreen State College Library, 1991). Available for $3.45 from The Evergreen State College Book Store.

NETWORKS AND ELECTRONIC ACCESS

Chapter 14

ELECTRONIC JOURNALS IN THE ACADEMIC LIBRARY

Suzanne Bell and Linda Coppola

INTRODUCTION

The electronic journal concept has quite a long history, most notably expressed by F.W. Lancaster in his Toward Paperless Information Systems.[1] There was no delay in practical implementations either, starting with the Electronic Information Exchange System experiment in 1978.[2] That experiment was quickly followed by the BLEND project sponsored by the Universities at Birmingham and Loughborough (UK) in 1980,[3] Learned Information's Electronic Magazine in 1984,[4] and Canada's Swift Current, also in 1984.[5] These first electronic journals were unique in that they were not digital replications of any existing print journals. Electronic versions of some print journals have been available "online" from commercial vendors such as Dialog, BRS, or Mead Data Central for many years, but only at significant expense.

However, we are now seeing a proliferation of a new version of the electronic journal. Like the early experiments, these electronic serials are not electronic versions of pre-existing print journals, and the subscription fees, if any, are nominal. (Most do not charge at all.) A major difference is that the current new crop of e-journals is available and distributed over the "public" networks, BITNET and Internet. All types of serial publications—

digests, newsletters, scholarly journals and magazines—are
represented in the array of journals springing up on the networks.

The e-journals now being distributed via BITNET and Internet
are also subtly different from previous efforts (we believe), just
because they are being presented to a rather different audience. In
an academic setting, it is almost a given that there will be a campus
computing department that supplies access to computing facilities
in individual labs or via a network available from anywhere on
campus or by dial-in. Computers are proliferating in libraries, in
the form of online catalogs, CD-ROM workstations, and,
increasingly, terminals for accessing the campus network. PCs,
Macs, and networked terminals are also appearing more frequently
in faculty and librarian offices.[6] More and more students arrive on
campus with some degree of computer expertise. In short, "there
now exists a critical mass of 'computer-literate' potential
subscribers" that are already accustomed to the idea that the
computer (like it or not!) is part of their academic life.[7] This
population may give electronic journals a warmer reception than
they have previously received.

Steadily improving technology has also played its part—even
the novice user can be assured of a remote access rate of at least
1200 baud, a reasonable monitor, and the benefits of sophisticated
but easy-to-use communications software. (The participants in the
BLEND project operating at 300 baud were real troopers!)[8] The
networks are also seeing advances in speed, protocol, and software
sophistication that make transferring lengthy texts the work of a
moment. The transmission of graphics and "image quality" pages
is dependent on hardware and software capabilities.

Beyond reflecting generally increasing computer awareness, the
recent efforts at producing and popularizing journals in an
electronic format have an added, economic impetus. Librarians
have been worrying in print for years about the rising cost of
serials,[9,10,11] but the current situation may truly be termed a crisis.
After years of trying to keep up, and only cutting one or two of
the priciest titles, the reduced buying power of existing serials
budgets has forced many libraries to cut subscriptions across the
board in hundred-thousand dollar increments. Then, too, there is
the issue of space, which is ultimately a matter of budget as well.[12]

Libraries' capacity for storing printed materials is reaching or, in many cases, has already reached its limits. If there is no money to build a bigger building—and there rarely is nowadays—what alternatives does a library have? The electronic format looks particularly attractive economically, and we believe libraries everywhere are anxious to note the progress of the e-journal—is it going to be The Answer? Only time will tell, of course. We hope that our experiences at Rochester Institute of Technology will help others understand some of the issues and encourage them to experiment.

WHAT'S OUT THERE?

There are many titles that are referred to as electronic serials, but the great majority of these are actually electronic bulletin boards or discussion groups where participants post inquiries or statements and readers comment or reply. True electronic journals do not have this "interactive" aspect, and we will not consider this type further. The first of the current wave of free or minimal cost electronic serials available over the "public" networks was probably *New Horizons in Adult Education*. This electronic journal was started in 1987 as a graduate student project at Syracuse University, and funded by a Kellogg grant. As initially conceived, *New Horizons* was to (a) provide a means for disseminating, via computer, current thinking within the field of adult education, (b) develop new avenues for connecting adult educators worldwide, and (c) generate dialogue among researchers and practitioners.[13] *New Horizons* has an editorial board that reviews the articles electronically before publication, and is currently indexed by ERIC. E-journals now seem to be appearing more and more rapidly: refereed, scholarly publications include *Psycoloquy*, 1989—, *Postmodern Culture*, 1990—, *Journal of the International Academy of Hospitality Research*, 1990—, *Electronic Journal of Communication/La Revue Electronique de Communication*, 1990—, and *E-journal*, 1991—.[14] *The Online Journal of Current Clinical Trials* appeared in July 1992, a joint effort of OCLC and the American Association for the Advancement of Science.[15,16] In another interesting development, the American Mathematical Society, with the assistance of the National Science Foundation, was planning to begin distribution of an electronic journal with mathematical formulas and graphics in the near future.[17] Those involved in publishing and using these journals have started meeting as the Association of Electronic Scholarly Journals, an indication of their seriousness and commitment.[18] There are a number of non-refereed but high quality e-journals available that are aimed at the library community: the *Public-Access Computer Systems Review*, the *Newsletter on Serials Pricing Issues*, and MeckJournal. Of general interest and popular content are e-journals such as *HICNet Newsletter* (MedNews -the Health Info-Com Network Newsletter; weekly medical news) and *Quanta-Science, Fact, and Fiction*.

The *Directory of Electronic Journals, Newsletters and Academic Discussion Lists,* compiled by Michael Strangelove and Diane Kovacs and published by the Association of Research Libraries in 1994, lists 181 of these publications. As with print journals, titles are being added and dropped continuously. Complete updated lists of electronic serials, in the form of online files, are maintained by Michael Strangelove at the University of Ottawa.[19] In addition, PACS-L, a computer conference on BITNET, publishes lists from time to time; backfiles of previous postings are also available.[20]

WHAT SHOULD BE IN YOUR COLLECTION?

Why would an institution decide that electronic journals merited a concerted effort to add them to the library collection? Usually engaging in a new format or the addition of a new service such as this involves a lengthy period of planning, discussion, budget, time, and staff allocations—in short, considerable struggle to implement. In addition, the BITNET/Internet e-journals currently available are a relatively recent development, have little track record, are generally not indexed, and they have little or no stature in the world of scholarly publishing; (i.e., being published in an e-journal carries nowhere near the weight of a publication in a traditional print journal in cases of promotion or tenure.)[21]

Indeed, is there enough of an audience for the e-journals to justify their inclusion?

In our case, the answers to all of these concerns were actually quite simple, due to a combination of circumstances:

- Our impetus came from informed sources at the top, rather than our having to convince an unwilling administration.
- Our campus computer system happens to provide a workable facility for loading e-journals.
- Faculty subscribers recommended titles to the library.

The RIT Library has a long history of being technologically oriented, and the current library director is an enthusiastic advocate of technological alternatives. Besides the director's own interest and knowledge, we have two other sources of information/ inspiration. RIT has an active and growing distance learning program, whose director is naturally very interested in any and all new developments that might benefit students working remotely. The distance learning program director and the library director both report to the same person, which helps ensure that new ideas that might benefit both parties get circulated. In addition, one of our history faculty is a very enthusiastic user and close monitor of new developments available on the networks. As he is blind, he uses an Archenstone PC with voice synthesizer to access the campus and global networks. This technology and network accessibility has made correspondence, teaching, reading newsletters and now journals as integral a part of his academic regime as such activities are for sighted faculty. He has often been our first source of information on new resources available electronically.

At the suggestion of these two colleagues, our director subscribed to the *Online Journal of Distance Education and Communication* when it was introduced several years ago, so she has been aware of the form for some time. However, only in the last couple of years have enough e-journals appeared on the networks to warrant seriously considering them as a form to affect collection development. In light of the current serials crisis (to which the renewed efforts to make a success of e-journals is almost certainly related), e-journals presented themselves as a "first baby step toward finding legitimate alternatives" in a situation where we are being "crippled and buried by serials price increases."[22]

IMPLEMENTING OUR E-JOURNAL COLLECTION

During a series of meetings of all Wallace Library department heads, responsibility for the various aspects of developing a collection of e-journals was apportioned and the implications explored. A committee was formed to handle the actual implementation.

Administration of the Project

Budget, usually the biggest issue in any new venture, turned out to be a minimal concern in this instance. Most of the e-journals on the networks are free; the few that do charge are very inexpensive. It was decided that the subscription fee for any that do charge would be initially paid for out of the director's discretionary funds. As the collection increases and more subject-specific titles are added, this may change, so that any subscription costs are charged against the serials budget for that subject. The cost in staff time, after the initial 'exploration' stage to determine how much time and effort would be involved, was and is not significant. In the current relationship between campus computing and the rest of the Institute, individual departments are not charged by the campus computing center for storage space, allowing the library to maintain and archive e-journals for free.

The committee chose *Postmodern Culture—PMC* to start the collection. It is a refereed journal, assuring a level of quality writing, and its wide-ranging topics would be of interest to a broad user population. In the pilot stages of the project, two subsequent titles, also of general interest, were also chosen by the committee: *HICNet Newsletter,* and *EJournal,* an electronic journal concerned with the implications of electronic documents and networks. As the collection is developed to include more subject-specific titles, the reference subject bibliographers will serve the same role for e-journals as for the traditional subscriptions in deciding which ones to acquire.

The Cataloging Manager handles issues pertaining to the cataloging of the new format, with the dual concerns of making sure the record on our OPAC is accurate and easily understood by patrons. Our e-journals are cataloged as serials, with the added element of putting directions for accessing the journal in the Notes field. There are already records for at least six electronic journals on OCLC, somewhat simplifying the process of creating catalog records for this new and unknown format. If original cataloging should be required, it now appears no more onerous than the cataloging of any other serial.[23]

The Library Systems department handles subscribing to the e-journals and getting them loaded to the campus computer system.

The RIT Computing Environment

The campus computing environment is the responsibility of Information Systems and Computing (ISC). ISC and the library both report to the same associate vice president, a situation that has facilitated useful coordination of several library/computing efforts. Access to computing resources is available from anywhere on campus—offices, computer labs, classrooms, the library—and by dial-in. The network, known collectively as RITVAX, is really a special group of five Digital VAX computers. What makes this group special is that the different machines are joined together to allow access to the same files, programs, and even some devices such as printers, from any member of the group. This arrangement is called a VAXcluster. The individual computers in the cluster vary in CPU type, memory, and speed, but the differences are largely invisible to users. Total memory available on the cluster is currently 464 megabytes; total disk space stands at 31.3 Gigabytes.

Computer accounts on the VAX system are available without charge to all faculty, staff, and registered students whether or not computer use is required in the student's program. Indeed, some faculty members from mathematics and the humanities incorporate use of electronic mail into their curriculum just because they have found it to be such an effective way to "reach" their students.

Software on the VAXcluster includes programs for word processing, statistics, graphics, programming languages, utilities, electronic mail, and much more. Of particular importance for the library's e-journal project is the 'conferencing' software on the VAXcluster known as Notes.

Notes Conferences

The Notes system is in some ways similar to electronic mail and/or electronic bulletin boards. Each "conference" is devoted to a particular topic, such as student-life or fitness. All conferences are moderated to some extent, meaning that each conference has one or more authorized person(s) who may review the contents of the conference and delete or re-arrange topics and replies. (Otherwise, entries may only be deleted by their authors.) The extent to which a conference is moderated simply reflects how much control the moderator feels a conference needs. A conference may be reserved for access only by members of a particular course, and serve as a forum for class discussion. In each case, topics are posted, either by the moderator or by conference subscribers, and those subscribing to the conference may read the topics and post their reply(s). Unlike some bulletin board systems, the Notes system has a fairly sophisticated user interface, and access occurs through a series of clear, formatted screens. All the topics that have been posted can be listed, as well as the replies to each topic. For example, suppose I add the conference on running to the set of conferences I subscribe to (my "notebook"). I can then open that conference, and list all the topics that have been posted since the conference was created. On any topics that look interesting (e.g., 4. Avoiding stitches), I can list the replies, read any that appeal, and add a reply of my own if I wish. The system is highly structured and yet friendly and interactive. The Notes system also presents an effective way to handle electronic journals: it was already in place, students and faculty were already familiar with it, and its structure helps make the journals easy to access and understand.

Therefore, a new Notes conference called Library—Journals was created through which the library could provide access to electronic journals. It is moderated by the Library's in-house programmer analyst, who subscribes to the electronic journals. When an issue arrives, he uses a text editor to remove the header and footer information added by the mail system, and loads the resulting file to the Notes conference. Library—Journals is a "read only" conference: campus subscribers may read the issues but cannot add any comments or replies. Each different electronic journal appears in the conference as a new Topic. For example, as we write the Library—Journals conference has four topics: an introduction and explanation, *Postmodern Culture*, the *HICNet Newsletter*, and *EJournal*. As issues of each e-journal arrive, they are posted as "replies" to their journal name/topic. Thus *Postmodern Culture*, a quarterly publication, only gets a new 'reply' posted every quarter. MedNews, a weekly published in four parts, accumulates replies at such a rate that only the more recent issues are kept active in the conference.

The Notes system includes a print command for making hardcopy output of any topic or reply. Topics or replies may also be downloaded to a user's personal account, using a SAVE command. The resulting files can then be edited, inserted into word processing documents, and so on. Our decision to experiment with developing a collection of e-journals was certainly made easier by the presence of the Notes conference system, a framework already in place and acceptable for loading the new format. However, several other technological set-ups would work equally well. It should be possible to adapt any similar network conferencing or bulletin board-type feature to handle e-journals. In the absence of a campus network, one micro with a modem in the library could be used to receive and download e-journals, as is the case at Michigan State University in East Lansing.[24] These might then be made available on a library LAN or just on the one machine. Some programming would probably be desirable to provide an easy interface for choosing the e-journal issue to be read (rather than having users rooting around in the directory and simply TYPEing issue-files they wished to see). In each case, the cost—of staff time and disk space—should not be insurmountable.

Metz & Gherman have also suggested that OCLC would be a good vehicle for supplying network access or delivery of e-journals to libraries that do not have an Internet connection.[25] Like RIT, Virginia Polytechnic Institute and State University (Virginia Tech), has a record on their online catalog for each electronic journal they subscribe to, with instructions for accessing the journals on the University LAN. Their OPAC record also includes a call number, so that the e-journals will appear in the same subject group with other hardcopy material as users search or browse the catalog. The e-journals (seven titles as of February 1992) are stored on the University mainframe, accessible through the same software system used for general library information and online transaction forms. For those e-journals that do not arrive in full text (such as *Postmodern Culture*), members of the Library Automation Division perform the extra step of retrieving the full text of each article. All articles are then posted on the University mainframe. In addition, they have also retrieved all back articles for their journal subscriptions. Future plans call for the Technical Services Division to assume all responsibilities for processing (ordering, receiving, cataloging, checkin, and posting) electronic journals. As to the question of archival storage, Virginia Tech is "committed to preserving these titles in their full form, online, until there is a commitment on a national scale to store and make them available into perpetuity." They do not plan to store any of the electronic journals in hardcopy form.[26]

Training and Promotion

Once the electronic journals had been added to VAX Notes the next concern was to make the community aware of them and how to use them. Promotion has been done on a variety of levels.

Information Systems and Computing (ISC) introduces all new conferences by listing them in an online directory on the VAX. The directory gives a synopsis of the conference, indicates who is eligible to receive it, who the moderator is, and directions for use. The Academic Computing and User Services department of ISC also runs a seminar series called "Making Friends With the VAX." This series has a core of eight one hour seminars dealing with various aspects of the VAX system. One is an introduction to the computer system for first time computer users; one is entitled "Why Use the Vax?" to attract the skeptics; four are "Getting Started" sessions that go into all the features of the system; one deals specifically with the Word Perfect word processing package; and the last one deals with electronic mail. This core is presented at least three times per quarter, year round. One session of the "Getting Started" group covers the basic how-to's of Notes conferencing. A separate seminar devoted to Notes conferences is offered once a year. People may attend the whole series, any individual seminar or any specialized seminar. Attendance varies per seminar and per time slot.[27]

Wallace Library promotes the e-journals in a number of ways. As mentioned above, e-journal listings appear in our OPAC as serial entries. Directions for accessing the e-journal in the Library—Journals Notes conference are provided in the Notes field of the OPAC record. Users who query the OPAC by title, keyword or subject are thus made aware of the library's collection of e-journals along with traditional printed materials.

Two library publications were initially used to promote electronic journals. "Yet Another Newsletter," the Wallace Library communique, regularly features new library services, as well as new holdings. This is distributed campus-wide. We also have an extensive collection of reference guides that feature special collections, provide how-to information and list new acquisitions. A guide, entitled "Electronic Conferences Sponsored by Wallace Library," explains the two Notes conferences that are available: the Wallace—Library conference (a forum for questions and discussion of any library-related issues), and the Library—Journals read-only electronic journals conference. This guide is available to all patrons and is distributed to all attendees of the Library's Noontime Seminar Series. Our seminar series, which is offered each quarter and twice in the Fall, is a four-part series highlighting services available electronically through the Library. It was originally designed as a one-time two- or three-hour session that ran twice each quarter. Each extended session tried to explain all our services as well as give a little history. It was too long and not very flexible. The revised series consists of four one-hour programs offered at lunchtime and open to all faculty, staff and students. The four seminars cover: (1) our OPAC ("Einstein"), electronic reference, and the Library Notes conferences, (2) the CD-ROM databases available in the library and on the VAX (we highlight different ones in each series), (3) the Dow Jones Retrieval Service, and (4) the CARL database and Internet connections to other library catalogs. A flyer is distributed campus-wide advertising the series, and copies are also posted throughout campus. Patrons who have attended these sessions have praised the library and staff and been amazed at the wealth of information available. However, most of the attendees have been faculty and staff and attendance has been declining. We are again in the process of re-evaluating the series to determine new ways of promoting to students, and changes in format that will attract a larger audience. Whatever changes are made, a discussion of electronic journal access will be included.

Lastly, the recent publicity connected with the completion of our building renovation has given us an opportunity to promote all of our library services in the campus news publications.

Within the library itself, in-house seminars are held to ensure that all staff who work at the reference desk are familiar with services available to patrons. Weekly reference staff meetings provide a very convenient forum for on-going training and refresher sessions. Staff from other departments who work the desk are given training sessions on new services as they become available.

ARCHIVING AND OTHER CONCERNS

Technological innovations, friendly computing techniques, and widespread network accessibility have contributed to the emerging acceptance of electronic journals as a legitimate method for the dissemination of information. Peer-review of submitted articles and indexing by major indexing services will also lend credibility to this format. The new organization formed in October 1990, the Association of Electronic Scholarly Journals, plans to address many unresolved issues related to electronic scholarly journals, especially the perceived barriers to their acceptance as a format on an equal footing with the traditional print journal. The association is made up of librarians, publishers and representatives of most of the dozen or so refereed electronic journals in existence or in planning. Some of the issues to be addressed are: copyright protection, volatility of the data and permanent archival storage, pagination, academic weight and value equal to print, and citation standards.[28]

These issues and other local issues are being discussed in committees at individual libraries as they begin making e-journals available to their patrons. Libraries need to make their thoughts/ decisions in these areas known in the literature and through discussion lists in order to ensure that others can make a more informed decision. For example, in December 1991 Wilfred Drew, Serials/Reference/Computer Librarian at SUNY College of Agriculture & Technology at Morrisville, NY put out a request on PACS-L for information on using VAX Notes for posting e-journals. We responded, as did 16 others, with our thoughts on how effectively the system worked. Mr. Drew posted several of the responses gathered along with his decision to go ahead with a pilot project. Many of the responses were enthusiastic but some were negative.[29] From this sort of exchange we gleaned bits of information on what others are doing, who is doing it and how. All of this can be useful in making or re-evaluating our own decisions. At RIT, our committee is looking at issues only as they become relevant to our situation. As mentioned earlier, our campus computing facility is able and willing to provide us with as much active disk storage space as the project currently requires. Although we are planning to add more titles in the near future, we do not project that this will make extreme demands on the storage capacity of the computing center. If we were to take up the policy of retrieving all the fulltext articles from those publications issued only in abstract form, then we might well exceed the limits of disk storage that the computing center can afford to give us. At that point we would evaluate the choices available for long term storage. We are thankful that for the next year or so it appears that we can continue to simply keep the e-journals on the VAXcluster, in "active" storage status.

The electronic storage alternative of downloading the e-journal files to magnetic tapes is possible, but not very appealing.

Archiving the files to tapes imposes another layer of inaccessibility for users: the problem of determining which tape, and then needing a computer operator load and run the tape, so that, eventually, for a limited time, the information is available. If the library does not have the facility for making, storing, and running their own tapes, this form of archiving becomes the complete responsibility of another department, a situation that may lead to problems of communication or material control.

Subscriptions to some of the electronic journals provide fiche copy for archival purposes and this is an option for libraries desiring a hands-on format. It is also possible to download to floppy disk and make that the archive. This has some advantages over downloading to tapes, in that it's much easier to identify which disk has the desired backfile, and the disks can be easily stored in the library. The disadvantage of using diskettes for archival purposes is their greater chance of being lost or damaged, and their volatility—the chance that they may simply "go bad" for no apparent reason.

Until libraries develop large collections, with multiple volumes, their methods for archiving past issues of electronic journals will vary. As collections grow, technology improves, and discussion becomes wide spread, we trust the archival issue will be resolved by consensus, and what works best will be used.

CONCLUSION

We will close with a few words of advice. The success of any format depends on its ease of use, its visibility, and its pertinence. Therefore, however you choose to load or store electronic journals, try to ensure that access is simple and available from as many places as possible. For those e-journals sent out in abstract form, having someone retrieve the full text of all the articles would probably be well worth it (as is done at VPI), if staff and computer storage permit. This saves the users from having to do that one extra step.[30] It also makes sense to have one central computer file of the article, rather than several users eating up their disk allowances with their own copies.

Next, make sure people know you have these electronic journals, and how to use them. Make sure faculty know what you have, and, if possible, work with the faculty to incorporate use of e-journals in their students' research. Go over e-journals in BI sessions, just as you do CD-ROMs, the OPAC, and so on. List them in library pathfinders along with traditional journals.

To make sure the e-journal collection is pertinent to researchers' needs, load a variety of titles. It might be most effective to get faculty and students' attention with a subject specific title. For example, the *Journal of the Academy of Hospitality Research* would probably be a very useful and interesting addition to a hotel and tourism program. The e-journals that deal with more general topics, such as *Postmodern Culture*, might present an avenue for pulling humanities faculty and students into use of this new form. Also, the collection needn't be all scholarly. Something like the *HICNet Newsletter* (MedNews), that provides short, timely bits of information on topics of general interest, could turn out to be the most popular of your e-journal titles. A newsletter also tends to appear more often, so that its content is dynamic and changing. If readers are checking the system weekly to see what's new on MedNews, they will become comfortable with the format, and may be more likely to also make use of the more academic e-journals.

Finally, e-journals are not perfect. Most people would rather read a paper version than view a screen, a whole human factors issue we have not attempted to address here. To be able to send and receive e-journals with graphics will require expenditures for better technology by senders and receivers. However, electronic journals also offer possibilities, and if libraries don't take them on, who will? Librarians' excellent skills at "imposing systematic coherence" can be well employed in "taming the unruly electronic environment." We can "help civilize the electronic media," organizing and making it comprehensible to others, so that electronic formats will truly provide "useful service to the research community."[31]

ACKNOWLEDGMENTS

Many thanks go to all the people who so patiently answered our questions and helped us get material for this chapter: in ISC, Dale B. Grady, and in Wallace Library, Patricia Pitkin, Marcia Trauernicht, Jonathan Millis, Sheila Simmons, and Wendy DiMatteo.

NOTES

1. F.W. Lancaster, *Toward Paperless Information Systems* (New York: Academic, 1978) as quoted in Neil A. Campbell, "On Paperless-ness," *Canadian Library Journal* 41 (August 1984): 181.

2. Murray Turoff and Starr Roxanne Hiltz, "The Electronic Journal: a Progress Report," *Journal of the American Society for Information Science* 33 (July 1982): 196-199.

3. B. Shackel, "An Overview of Research on Electronic Journals," in *Cognitive Engineering in the Design of Human Computer Interaction and Expert Systems*, ed. G. Salvendy (Amsterdam: Elsevier Science Publishers, 1987): 200-202.

4. Harry R. Collier, "Learned Information's Electronic Magazine: a Case Study," *Serials Review* 12 (Summer/Fall 1986): 70.

5. Rumi Yamamoto, "Another Interface: Electronic Publishing and Technical Services," *Canadian Library Journal* 43 (August 1986): 238-239.

6. Patricia Ohl Rice, "From Acquisitions to Access," *Library Acquisitions: Practice & Theory* 14 (1991): 19.

7. Czeslaw Jan Grycz, "The Future of Serials Librarianship," *Serials Review* 16 (Summer 1990): 57.

8. B. Shackel, "The BLEND System: Programme for the Study of Some 'Electronic Journals'," *Journal of the American Society for Information Science* 34 (January 1983): 28.

9. Neil A. Campbell, "On Paperless-ness," *Canadian Library Journal* 41 (August 1984): 182.

10. Eldred Smith, "Resolving the Acquisitions Dilemma: Into the Electronic Information Environment," *College & Research Libraries* 52 (May 1991): 231-232.

11. Clifford A. Lynch, "Serials Management in the Age of Electronic Access," *Serials Review* 17 (Spring 1991): 7-8.

12. Paul Metz and Paul M. Gherman, "Serials Pricing and the Role of the Electronic Journal," *College & Research Libraries* 52 (July 1991): 324.

13. Michael Ehringhaus, *The Electronic Journal: Promises and Predicaments*, ERIC Document ED 316 732 (February 1990): 11-13.

14. David L. Wilson, "Testing Time for Electronic Journals," *The Chronicle of Higher Education* (September 11, 1991): A24.

15. OCLC, "OCLC and the American Association for the Advancement of Science Develop New Online Journal," news release (24 September 1991): 1-2.

16. Martin Wilson, "AAAS Plans Electronic Journal Venture with OCLC," *Information Today* (November 1991): 19.

17. Wilson, "Testing Time," A24.

18. Margaret Morrison, "Electronic Scholarly Journals," *Information Standards Quarterly* 3 (January 1991): 9.

19. These may be obtained by sending the following commands in an electronic mail message to LISTSERV@UOTTAWA:
GET EJOURNL1 DIRECTRY   GET EJOURNL2 DIRECTRY

20. To join PACS-L, send an electronic mail message to LISTSERV@U-HUPVM1 that says: SUBSCRIBE PACS-L Firstname Lastname.

21. Wilson, "Testing Time," A24.

22. Patricia Pitkin, R.I.T., Electronic mail message to authors, 29 October 1991.

23. Marcia Trauernicht, R.I.T., Electronic mail message to authors, 29 October 1991.

24. Jeannette Fiore, Michigan State University at East Lansing, Phone interview with author, 19 December 1991.

25. Metz and Gherman, "Serials Pricing," 325-326.

26. Charles A. Litchfield, Chief, Library Automation Division, Virginia Tech. Libraries, Electronic mail messages to author, 23 December 1991.

27. Dale B. Grady, Electronic mail message to author, 7 January 1992.

28. Morrison, "Electronic Scholarly Journals," 10.

29. Wilfred Drew, "VAX Notes and e-journals," Message on PACS-L@UHUPVM1 computer conference, Bitnet, 13 January 1992.

30. The situation at RIT is far from ideal, as revealed by this progression: see entry on the catalog --> find a terminal with access to the Vax --> get into Notes, add Library—Journals to personal Notebook --> read replies (issues) of journals --> for those that only send abstracts, note the article reference --> leave Notes --> get into Mail, and send a message requesting the full text of the desired article. Whew!

31. Grycz, "Future of Serials Librarianship," 59.

SUPPLEMENTAL BIBLIOGRAPHY

"ALA's First Electronic Newsletter Available Via ALANET." *Library Journal*, 15 November 1989, 25.

Arnold, Stephen E. "Storage Technology: A Review of Options and Their Implications for Electronic Publishing." *Online* 15(July 1991):39-50.

Astle, Deana L. "The Scholarly Journal: Whence or Wither." *Journal of Academic Librarianship* 15(July 1989):151-156.

Auld, Larry. "Reader Interaction with the Online Journal." *Serials Review* 12(Summer/Fall 1986):83-85.

Bailey, Charles W., Jr. "Electronic Serials on BITNET." *Computers in Libraries* 11(April 1991):50.

Bailey, Charles W., Jr. "Electronic (Online) Publishing in Action...The Public-Access Computer Systems Review and Other Electronic Serials." *Online* 15(January 1991): 28-35.

Butler, Brett. "Scholarly Journals, Electronic Publishing, and Library Networks." *Serials Review* 12(Summer/Fall 1986): 47-52.

Calabrese, Andrew M. *The Electronic Journal: A Review of Trends and Their Implications for Scholarly Communication.* ERIC Document ED 278 076, April 1986.

Case, Donald. "The Personal Computer: Missing Link to the Electronic Journal?" *Journal of the American Society for Information Science* 36(September 1985): 309-313.

DeLoughry, Thomas J. "Scholarly Journals in Electronic Form Seen as Means to Speed Pace of Publication and Promote Dialogue." *The Chronicle of Higher Education,* 22 March 1989.

Directory of Electronic Journals, Newsletters and Academic Discussion Lists. Washington, DC: Association of Research Libraries, Office of Scientific and Academic Publishing, 1991.

Dodd, W.P. "Convergent Publication, or the Hybrid Journal: Paper Plus Telecommunications." *Electronic Publishing* 3(February 1990): 47-59.

Freeman, David T. "The False Start of the Electronic Journal: A Look at Human Factors and Automation." In *Information: The Transformation of Society.* ASIS '87: Proceedings of the 50th Annual Meeting of the American Society for Information Science, edited by Ching-chih Chen, 79-82. Medford, NJ: Learned Information, 1987.

Johnson, Peggy. "Electronic Scholarly Communications." *Technicalities* 10(June 1990): 4-7.

Morasch, Bruce. "Electronic Social Psychology." *Serials Review* 12 (Summer/Fall 1986): 113-116.

Okerson, Ann. "Accessing Electronic Journals: A Survey of Canadian and American Libraries." *The Serials Librarian* 15, no. 3/4(1988):73-83.

Perry, Brian J. "The Impact of Electronic Publishing on Library Collection and Services: A British View." In *IFLA General Conference, 1987.* Division of Collections and Services. Interlending and Document Delivery Section.

Serial Publications Section. *Papers.* ERIC Document ED 299 995, August 1987.

Piternick, Anne B. "Attempts to Find Alternatives to the Scientific Journal: A Brief Review." *The Journal of Academic Librarianship* 15(November 1989):260-266.

Piternick, Anne B. "Serials and New Technology: The State of the 'Electronic Journal.'" *Canadian Library Journal* 46 (April 1989):93-97.

Sabosik, Patricia E. "Electronic Subscriptions." *The Serials Librarian* 19, no. 3-4(1991):59-70.

Yavarkovsky, Jerome. "A University-Based Electronic Publishing Network." *EDUCOM Review* 25 (Fall 1990):14-20.

Zahray, W. Paul, and Marvin Sirbu. "The Provision of Scholarly Journals by Libraries Via Electronic Technology: An Economic Analysis." *Information Economics and Policy* 4(1989/90):127-154.

Chapter 15

TRAINING LIBRARIANS TO NETWORK

PART I. OPACS ON THE INTERNET: A HOW-TO GUIDE

Billy Barron

PART II. TRAINING ON THE INTERNET: A PERSONAL VIEW

Peter Scott

PART I. OPACs ON THE INTERNET: A HOW-TO GUIDE

This chapter will look at a variety of technical details from the novice's point of view. These details include a history of the Internet, connection procedures, and the searching of OPACs (Online Public Access Catalogs). It should be noted that since computer networking is a rapidly changing field, some of the information within this chapter may quickly become obsolete. (*Editor's note:* This chapter was written in July 1992.)

The Internet

In 1968, an early computer network known as the ARPANET (Advanced Research Projects Agency NETwork) was developed. Many defense contractors needed the same kinds of computer resources so ARPA, a branch of the United States Department of Defense (DOD), built the ARPANET which was an overwhelming success. Then in 1983, a part of the ARPANET was broken off and became MILNET. However, as far as users were concerned, it still appeared as one network. This was the beginning of the Internet, which is a collection of many computer networks that are interconnected and appear as one network to the user. Between 1983 and 1992, many new networks became important parts of the Internet, for instance the NSFNET (National Science Foundation NETwork) and ESNET (Energy Sciences NETwork). In June 1992 the Internet Society reported that the global network is made up of 7,500 separate networks with four million users connecting through one million computers.[1]

Though the network is made up of many parts, academic libraries are usually connected to the NSFNET portion of the Internet in the United States or to the national network in most other countries. In addition, other networks, such as JANET (Joint Academic NETwork), are accessible via gateways. For librarians, JANET is among the more important ones as many UK libraries are on it. Other networks not connected to the Internet, such as the European IXI network, have OPACs available over them also.

The Internet currently uses the TCP/IP (Transmission Control Protocol/Internet Protocol) protocol suite. Over the next several years, it may migrate over to the OSI (Open Systems Interconnect) protocol suite. However, most people agree that TCP/IP is so prevalent today that it will take 20 to 30 years to be totally phased out, if at all. The transition time should be interesting for computer networking although it may at times be painful for users. OSI is only routed across the NSFNET backbone on a test basis as this is being written. It will take some time after it is routed in a production fashion for library applications to use the new OSI protocols. Therefore, the rest of this chapter will concentrate on the TCP/IP portion of the network.

OPACs on the Internet

The OPACs on the Internet are valuable resources for both librarians and other academics. Typical users outside of the library in academic environments include faculty, researchers, and graduate students.

Library Uses:

- Different search capabilities are available on other library systems. This may allow for easier identification of materials than the local system can provide.
- The Internet gives the ability to search when the local system is down provided network access is still up or a dial-in is possible.
- Librarians can coordinate cooperative collection development.
- Librarians can answer reference questions using specialized indices or databases that are available over the network.
- Librarians can gain a new outlook by becoming a "new user" on another system.
- Information from national services, such as OCLC and RLIN, can be double checked with local information because in some cases the local information is more accurate.
- Librarians can access RLIN and OCLC's EPIC databases over the network.
- Libraries without OCLC or RLIN can still find books for Interlibrary Loan.
- Citations and information for acquisitions can be verified over the network.
- Catalogers can review how other libraries have listed materials.
- Libraries searching for replacement automated cataloging systems can see how other systems operate.

Research Uses:

- Researchers can find new and unique materials from around the world.
- Researchers can prepare for research trips to other libraries. The location of needed works can be determined in advance. Also, the trip is not wasted if the local computer system goes down while there, because call numbers are in hand.

- Academics who are thinking of changing schools can check other libraries' holdings in their field of study before making their decision.
- Grant administrators who need information about whether to fund a grant proposal may be able to verify the strength of the applicant's library holdings in the proposed area.
- Users can access remote full-text services. This includes both free and pay-for-use services (e.g., CARL's Uncover).
- Users can use regional information, such as local newspapers, that may be available online elsewhere in either an index or full-text format.
- Instructors can teach users the basics of information retrieval using different systems.
- Researchers can search other libraries for materials that they wish to get through Interlibrary Loan.
- Researchers working on collaborative projects can check each other's holdings for references.

Connecting to the Internet

Though on the surface, connecting to the network seems like a simple procedure, it is potentially the most difficult part of the whole process. If you have a central computing organization, start by talking with them. In many cases, the Internet will already be on campus, and then it is just a matter of extending it to your location on campus. If your site has no central computing organization, start by contacting your regional NSFNET network in the United States or your national network in other countries. *The Matrix* by John S. Quarterman[2] and *!% ¢:, A Directory of Electronic Mail Addressing and Networks* by Donnalyn Frey and Rick Adams[3] contain information on the various networks and how to contact them.

If you do not have a regional or national network covering your area, then services, such as ANS, Alternet, and PSINET, are willing to sell you connections to the Internet. Please note that other networks, such as BITNET, Fidonet, and UUCP, while they are valuable in their own way and are able to exchange electronic mail with the Internet, are not part of the Internet and will not provide you with the OPAC services described in this chapter. A few networks such as the UK's JANET have an interactive gateway to the Internet. In these cases, make sure before connecting that the gateway supports at least TELNET and preferably TN3270.

The actual technical detail of connecting to the Internet is dependent on your individual situation. This chapter will not attempt to describe the possible steps here, as it is best determined by you and the people helping you connect up.

Access to Other OPACs

To access other academic libraries across the Internet, you must first find out the library's Internet address. Fortunately, some free electronic guides containing this information are available. They are listed along with instructions on how to acquire them near the end of this chapter.

Internet nodenames look something like samba.acs.unc.edu. These names are hierarchical in structure. Reading backwards, we first find "edu" which means educational. Next we have "unc" which is the University of North Carolina. "acs" in this case stands for Academic Computing Services. Finally, "samba" is the name of the computer itself. These names exist only for convenience. Most computers are able to translate the names into numeric addresses which are four numbers separated by periods like 129.120.2.4. If you are using a computer system that does not handle the translation, then you must use the numeric addresses. The numeric addresses are listed in the library addresses document described later in this chapter.

For remote login purposes, in most cases, the Internet is divided in two types of computers: line mode and full screen computers. The line mode computers display lines or characters at a time. Some examples of these are VAXes, UNIX, and microcomputers. The full screen systems display a whole screen at a time and are typically only found on IBM mainframe systems. It is important to determine which type you are using. Clues like VT100, VT52, VT220, VT320, ANSI, or TTY usually mean line mode, and 3270 usually means full screen.

Line Mode vs. Full Screen Computers

Line mode computers connect to other line mode computers, or IBM mainframes that have a front-end device called a protocol converter, using a command known as TELNET. On most systems, the syntax is "TELNET <internet-nodename>."

Not all line mode computers are able to connect to full screen IBM mainframe systems. Those that can use the TN3270 command. The syntax is "TN3270 <internet-nodename>."

To connect to another full screen system, the TELNET command is used by the command "TELNET <internet-nodename>." This TELNET command is similar to the TN3270 command used by line mode systems.

Connecting from a full screen system to a line mode system is very problematic. Without the purchase of some extra third party products, it is, for all practical purposes, unfeasible and even then it is quite limited.

The guides to accessing OPACs are designed for the users of line mode computers. However, it is simple to interpolate the directions if you use a full screen system. Basically, replace the word "TN3270" with "TELNET." Also, if the directions say "TELNET," then you can try "TELNET nodename (L." Though it does not always work and is usually ugly when it does, it is better than nothing.

Searching

Each library OPAC software package is different in terms of its user interface. Some of the packages (e.g., Innovative Interfaces) allow customization of the interface. In some cases, the library may even be in a different language though many allow you to switch languages. Also, different libraries list different materials. To effectively use the various systems, you will need to get used to these differences.

The catalogs are either menu-driven or command-driven. Menu-driven systems are usually easier to use, but they are often less flexible. Different menu-driven systems may structure their menus in different ways. The variances of the command-driven interfaces are typically much greater. Major packages such as VTLS, NOTIS, and GEAC each have their own unique querying language. A Common Command Language standard (NISO Z39.58) has been created, and many vendors are making their products conform to this standard. This will allow the same command to be used across many packages.

Each OPAC on the Internet has slightly different bibliographic content. Collections vary. Some libraries have converted their entire card catalog to machine-readable formats, although most have only a portion online. Typically, the part that is online includes newer materials and materials that have circulated since the online system has been in existence. Some OPACs have books, but no journals listed. Others have both. Of the libraries that have both, some allow simultaneous searching of different materials. However, others will require multiple search commands.

Information on the Internet OPACs

Many sources of information for Internet OPACs are available as files on the Internet. I will describe only a few of the sources, even though many more exist. These are primary sources which will hopefully continue to be maintained for years to come. It should be noted that all the information is compiled by volunteers, much of whose spare time is devoted to indexing the Internet for the benefit of other users. For announcements of updated versions of the resources it is recommended that a user subscribe to such electronic mailing-lists as PACS-L and LIB—HYTELNET.

Individual documents for certain countries exist, but "Accessing Online Bibliographic Databases" that I edit contains worldwide information and is frequently updated.[4]

Hypertext Sources

For MS-DOS, UNIX and VMS users, the HYTELNET package presents this information in an easy-to-search online fashion. The MS-DOS version by Peter Scott is a TSR (Terminate, Stay, Resident) program that can be called up on the screen at any time. The UNIX and VMS versions by Earl Fogel of the University of

Saskatchewan uses the information files from the MS-DOS version. These are stand alone programs. The Macintosh, UNIX, and VMS versions support automatic connections to the OPACs without the user having to type in the TELNET and TN3270 commands themselves. CATALIST is a hypertext program for MS-Windows that includes the library information.

Acquiring Information from an Internet Site

To acquire these documents follow the instructions below. Note that they are for Internet sites only.

To Retrieve

At your system prompt, enter:
> **FTP FTP.UNT.EDU**

When you receive the Name prompt, enter:
> **ANONYMOUS**

When you receive the password prompt, enter:
> your Internet address

When you are at the ftp > prompt, enter:
> **BINARY** [only if you need binary mode]

At the next ftp > prompt, enter:
> **CD LIBRARY** [or cd library/catalist for CATALIST].

Then enter:
GET filename
(Note: A list of possible filenames follows the BITNET instructions.)

Acquiring Information from a BITNET Only Site

Users with access only to BITNET, not the Internet, should send a mail message to BITFTP@PUCC with HELP as the first and only line of the message. The response will give you instructions on using the Princeton BITFTP server, which provides a mail interface to the FTP portion of the TCP/IP protocol suite.

To use BITFTP, send mail to BITFTP@PUCC.BITNET. The body should be as follows:

At your system prompt, enter:

> FTP FTP.UNT.EDU [filetype]
> USER ANONYMOUS
> your-e-mail-address
> CD LIBRARY
> BINARY {only if it is a binary file like WordPerfect}
> GET filename
> QUIT

Filetype is the either blank for text, UUENCODE for a UUENCODED version of the file (need UUDECODE to undo), or NETDATA for IBM NETDATA format (may only work for IBM Mainframe BITNET users).

Filenames

A list of available filenames follows:

Files	*Filename*
ASCII/Text version	LIBRARIES.TXT
Postscript	LIBRARIES.PS
WordPerfect	LIBRARIES.WP5 {must be transferred in BINARY}
	LIBRARIES.CON {must be transferred in BINARY}
Contacts file	LIBRARIES.CONTACTS
Numeric IP Address File	LIBRARIES.ADR
HYTELNET (MS-DOS)	HYTELNnn.ZIP {must be transferred in BINARY}
HYTELNET (VMS/ UNIX)	HYTELNET.SH
CATALIST	CAT10.EXE {must be transferred in BINARY}
	FULLCAT.EXE {must be transferred in BINARY} README.TXT

The nn in the HYTELNET filename is the version number. For example, HYTELN62.ZIP is version 6.2.

Conclusion

Since the field of computer networking is developing at an astounding rate the future will hold many changes in the next few years for computer networking and libraries. Unfortunately, the changes could make this chapter quickly obsolete.

Currently most sites connect to the Internet at a fixed rate; however, discussion is in progress about usage based charges. Usage based charges will greatly affect the way the Internet is deployed. The implementation of such charges has yet to be determined and many voices will participate in this discussion, including librarians.

Transparent searching is a technology that is on the horizon. Instead of connecting to each site manually to search it, you will be able to search many OPACs at once from within your own OPAC. Your OPAC will make connections to other OPACs transparently as needed. This technology is in its infancy, and it is likely that we will not see wide scale implementation for at least another five years.

Finally, some systems, such as CARL's Uncover, Wide Area Information Services (WAIS), the University of Minnesota's Gopher, and WorldWideWeb (WWW) are newly released and provide full-text searching and retrieval of documents over the Internet. We should see more and more of these systems becoming available. Some, such as Uncover cost money, while others, such as WAIS, are free.

PART II.   TRAINING ON THE INTERNET: A PERSONAL VIEW

Most librarians employed by academic libraries have access to the Internet through computer accounts, but few actually take full advantage of the services available. This is an unfortunate situation, given that librarians need to be at the forefront of information services, not only as caretakers, but also as disseminators. These days, understanding the Internet, and using it to its full potential, is becoming mandatory in academic libraries.

Given this, the question now arises as to who is to take on the task of explaining the Internet and helping people to use it. Some libraries have a librarian devoted full time to such work. Others rely upon a local guru, who is personally, but not professionally, interested. Others use the services of a non-librarian staff member who may have a personal interest and is willing to share knowledge. Some libraries leave all training in the hands of the Computer Services Department. Unfortunately, in many cases, the Computer Services Department does not understand some of the complex issues that pertain to library uses.

Let's look at my own experience as a non-librarian with a keen interest in all aspects on the Internet. I gained access to all Internet services when our University, as part of Sask-Net, joined CA-Net, and subsequently the Internet. My former position was to run the monograph acquisitions unit. One of the main aspects of the job was to ensure that bibliographic information was verified before sending a firm order to a supplier. We had all the traditional tools for this function, but because many were paper sources, and out of date as soon as they were published, they were of little help in certain cases, particularly for non-North American publications. I had heard that there was some service on something called the Internet which allowed a person to log in to other libraries catalogs to perform searches. This struck me as a good idea, well worth pursuing. After a few abortive attempts, I managed to connect to CARL, the Colorado Alliance of Research Libraries. I was instantly amazed and spent many hours searching the various databases and other library catalogs available on the system. That experience led me to wonder what else was available to me. I began to ask questions and explore.

The first step was to join some Internet discussion groups, for example PACS-L, the Public Access Computer Systems list. The first group of messages I received concerned a debate about two lists of Internet-accessible libraries, one written by Billy Barron and the other by Art St. George. I managed to get hold of copies of these lists and was once again amazed to see how many other libraries were so accessible. I tried them all, and was, for a good deal of time, frustrated because I encountered terminology which meant absolutely nothing to me, for instance "TN3270," "Telnet escape key," and so on. Not one to give up easily, I decided to ask more questions, this time not from local people, but of the new colleagues I had found on the Internet.

In the meantime I had learned quite a bit more about the MAIL program on our VAX minicomputer and decided to turn the help screens, which I found most cumbersome, into a hypertext utility to run on my PC. This would give me and others instant help when needed, without having to leave mail in progress. It also struck me that a directory of Internet-accessible sites would also be an ideal candidate for such treatment, so I eagerly set about this task and created the first version of HYTELNET. This utility, now at version 6.2, is in use on hundreds of computers worldwide and allows new users to save themselves the trouble I had when first connecting to remote sites. I have also set up a mailing list called LIB—HYTELNET, which permits users to share information on new/changed/defunct Internet-accessible sites.

Since we have no "official" Internet trainer in the library I have assumed the role of unofficial trainer. I use much of my training session time showing people what is available to them on the Internet. I do this by running my HYTELNET utility, and pointing out all the various and unique sites to which they have access. These sites include not only other library catalogs but campus-wide information systems, bulletin boards, Freenets, full-text databases, and powerful searching systems. Add to that certain features of MAIL, including electronic journal subscriptions, messaging systems, Usenet news, and file transfer protocols, and a session participant will receive a good all-round view of the Internet.

I also like participants to have hands-on experience with MAIL, TELNET, and FTP, and have set up an account for such training purposes. During the course of a training session I ask participants if they have a particular interest which the Internet can address, or if they have a need to discover a site or messaging system which can answer a question a patron may have posed. This can certainly show off the power of the Internet, but it also requires that the trainer is keeping abreast of all the innovations occurring daily.

To keep people interested in what is happening on the network I frequently post relevant information on our electronic bulletin boards. This may be in form of a message from a Usenet news group, an Internet mailing list, or an issue of an electronic journal. The messages quite often pique the readers' imaginations and persuade them to pursue more sources of information.

Two final points about training follow. If anyone is contemplating setting up sessions to explore Internet resources, I would strongly suggest that the presentations be lively, contain as little "jargon" as possible, and that a trainer be prepared to answer all kinds of questions during a session. I would also urge a trainer to explain that once a user obtains access, he or she becomes a member of an ever-increasing "family" of colleagues who can be called upon at any time to help with questions, and to share information. The Internet is not static, and needs everyone's participation to grow and to provide more of the kinds of services that today's librarian requires.

ACKNOWLEDGMENTS

The authors wish to acknowledge the following people: Dr. Philip Baczewski and Claudia Lynch of UNT Academic Computing Services for their support; Roy Tennant for his aid with the FTP instructions contained within.

NOTES

1. *Chronicle of Higher Education* 38, no. 46 (July 23, 1992): A15.
2. John S. Quarterman, *The Matrix: Computer Networks and Conferencing Systems Worldwide* (Bedford, MA:Digital Press, 1990).
3. Donnalyn Frey and Rick Adams, *!% ‹:, A Directory of Electronic Mail Addressing and Networks* (Sebastopol, CA: O'Reilly & Associates, 1990).

SUPPLEMENTAL BIBLIOGRAPHY

Barron, Billy. (1991) "Another Use of the Internet: Libraries' Online Catalogs." *ConneXions: The Interoperability Report* 5, no 7 (1991): 15-19.
Farley, Laine. *Library Resources on the Internet: Strategies for Selection and Use.* RASD Occasional Papers, no. 12. Chicago: American Library Association, 1992.

Chapter 16

ELECTRONIC DISCUSSION GROUPS: A PRIMER[1]

Philip C. Baczewski

MAILING LISTS AND NEWS GROUPS

BITNET, the Internet, and other national and international networks are changing the way people acquire, assimilate, and act upon information. For some, "unplugging" the wide-area network would have almost as great a negative impact as would shutting off the electricity. It is possible to survive, but a great deal of powerful, time-saving technology would be unavailable. Networks have the unique ability to bring information on a wide variety of topics to a diverse group of people. Information is disseminated much more quickly than by traditional print methods. The information is available from a wider range of sources. There are two primary formats for distributing this information: mailing lists allow the distribution of electronic mail messages to a group of people sharing a similar interest; discussion groups are collections of online messages sometimes organized in topical hierarchies. Two wide-area networks have been responsible for bringing such resources into the academic realm: BITNET has fostered the growth of electronic mailing lists, while the Internet has contributed to the popularity of online discussion groups.

A reflection of the growth and impact of BITNET mailing lists can be found in the number and nature of the mailing list topics listed in a file called LISTSERV GROUPS, maintained at the

BITNET Network Information Center (BITNIC). In 1987, there were about 93 lists documented in LISTSERV GROUPS and of the ones which were not directly related to the BITNET network itself, 35 percent were on topics not directly related to computing. In a 1991 version of that file, the number of lists had grown to about 144, thirty-eight percent of which were on topics not directly related to computing, with a much more diverse set of disciplines represented. Today, there are over 3000 LISTSERV mailing lists in existence, with new lists being added every day. The majority of the new lists have nothing to do with computing, but are very much centered around academic and social topics. The word about BITNET is obviously spreading to more and more fields, and not just scientific disciplines. List topics include genealogy, the humanities, philosophy, intercultural and interpersonal communication, teaching English, health issues, environmental issues, and, of course, library and information sciences.

A similar growth pattern can also be seen for the Internet, which has become accessible to more and more academic institutions via regional networks funded by the National Science Foundation. A great number of mailing lists are maintained on the Internet. At the same time, access to the Internet has also encouraged rapid growth of USENET (USErs' NETwork). USENET is a wide-ranging collection of discussion groups whose messages are distributed by a number of means over a great number of national and international networks, commercial and educational. Sometimes you will hear USENET referred to as "USENET news" or "network news." This is because messages are conveyed by a different distribution method than are electronic mailing list messages and are usually accessed by specialized programs called "news readers."

This discussion will not go into great detail about the workings of BITNET or the Internet, but instead will concentrate on mailing lists and discussion groups. To take advantage of this information you will first need access to a computing system that is connected to one of these networks. You will also need to gain some working knowledge of that system to be able to sign on, edit and manipulate files, and, most importantly, send and receive electronic mail. The resources central to this discussion will be mailing lists maintained under BITNET LISTSERV installations and USENET discussion groups.

GETTING ON THE LISTS

In recent years, the words "mailing list" have taken on a most negative connotation in relation to the U.S. mails. People, when hearing the words "mailing list" immediately think the other two words, "junk mail." Unlike their surface mail counterparts, wide area network mailing lists carry quite positive connotations. Mailing lists allow you to establish communications with groups of people in the Unites States and around the world who share your same interest in a particular subject. Mailing lists can ensure the delivery of electronic magazines and other materials on general or special topics. Best of all, you choose the network mailing lists on which you will be included. Like their surface mail counterparts, however, network mailing lists can make trips to your electronic mail box rather overwhelming if the selection and use of those lists is not well managed. Included here are a few tips which will, hopefully, make your use of mailing lists as effective and enjoyable as possible.

Information about mailing lists is available from numerous sources including references from colleagues, announcements on existing electronic forums, professional newsletters, and so forth. In order to make the most efficient use of these resources, if you find a list that is of interest, make note of the following information:

Subscription Address. In the case of BITNET's LISTSERV facilities, subscription commands can be sent to the particular LISTSERV installation that maintains the list.

List Format. Some mailing lists "broadcast" all messages sent to it, while on others, a list moderator places the messages into digest form before they are sent to you. Digest mailing lists usually generate much less mail traffic than their "undigested" counterparts.

List Distribution. One piece of information often available is the various LISTSERVs at which a particular list is maintained. In general, the more sites at which a list is maintained, the more popular that list is, and therefore, the more mail traffic it will generate.

List Moderator. Most list descriptions include the name of the moderator and the moderator's network mailing address. Whether you subscribe to a list or not, the moderator can sometimes be helpful in providing additional information about that list, or suggesting alternate sources of information.

Once you absorb the note information, accessing network mailing lists can be quite simple. You may find, however, that managing all the mail generated from those lists can get to be a bit complex. Whenever possible, you should take advantage of a news reader program, which maintains subscriptions to many mailing lists and discussion groups. From a news reader, you can read and reply to these messages as if you had your own subscription. If you do subscribe to mailing lists individually, the following guidelines may be helpful for managing your list mail.

Limit Your Subscriptions. Two or three active lists may generate as much information as you can easily assimilate. Limit your subscriptions to those lists which provide you with the best information on your topics of most interest.

Read Your Mail Often. Mailing lists generate a continual stream of messages. If you don't read them often, they just stack up and occupy valuable system storage space. On most lists, mail is of immediate topical interest, and like leftovers in the refrigerator, may soon become quite useless (if not unappetizing) if left unassimilated.

Un-subscribe When You Will Be Away If you will be away from your network access and can't read your mail for even as little as a week, it is a good idea to sign off from your mailing lists. (Remember that all BITNET LISTSERV subscription and sign-off commands should be sent to a

LISTSERV, i.e., LISTSERV@nodename, rather than the list, i.e., listname@nodename—see "Using LISTSERV," below). A week's worth of messages from an active list may continually keep you in "catch-up" mode.

INTERNET MAILING LISTS

Internet-based mailing lists are usually not maintained using the LISTSERV program which is so common on BITNET. If you see a reference for an Internet mailing list, it will often list an address to which subscription addresses can be sent. Sometimes the address is that of the list moderator and other times it is a special address. Check the list description carefully for subscription instructions and, more importantly, note and save any instructions for unsubscribing from the list.

USING LISTSERV

Subscribing

Once you have decided to explore electronic mailing lists and discussion groups, the first step is to subscribe to a particular list. The same basic command can be used to subscribe to any BITNET LISTSERV mailing list: SUB <listname> <your name> where SUB stands for "subscribe," <listname> is the name of the mailing list, and <your name> is your first and last name. You don't have to specify your network address, since it is automatically contained in the message you will send to subscribe. The tricky part is knowing how and where to send this command.

First the "how" part: the subscribe command can be sent as an interactive message from a VAX or CMS system connected to BITNET, and can be sent as the first line of a mail message from any computing system connected to BITNET or the Internet. Now the "where" part: most BITNET mailing lists are referred to in the form of a BITNET address with the format <listname>@<node>. Since mailing lists are almost always maintained by a LISTSERV installation, your subscribe command should be sent to LISTSERV<node>, where LISTSERV is the user-id portion of the BITNET address and <node> is the node found as part of the list specification. Sometimes, you only know the list name and not its associated node. All is not lost, however, since most LISTSERVs on BITNET know about all other LISTSERVs and the mailing lists they maintain. This means that you can send your subscribe command to the nearest LISTSERV and it will forward your request to the appropriate installation.

So, to subscribe to a mailing list from a VAX system, use:
SEND LISTSERV@<node> SUB <listname> <your name> from a CMS system:
TELL LISTSERV@<node> SUB <listname> <your name>
Or on any system connected to BITNET or the Internet send a mail message to: LISTSERV@<node> with the line SUB <listname> <your name> as the first line of the mail message.

Signing Off

The other important piece of information needed when working with LISTSERV mailing lists is how to sign off. If you decide to discontinue reading a list, go out of town for a week or more, or move to another institution, you will need to temporarily or permanently sign off of you BITNET lists. The command to stop a BITNET LISTSERV subscription is SIGNOFF <listname>. This command must be sent to the appropriate LISTSERV (see above) via either an interactive message or as the first line of a mail message. If you are going to be away and unable to read your BITNET mail for any length of time, it is a good idea to sign off of all of your BITNET mailing list subscriptions. This can be accomplished with one command sent to the nearest LISTSERV:
SIGNOFF * (NETWIDE
meaning, sign off of all mailings lists subscribed to, anywhere on BITNET. However, since this command generates a large number of message on BITNET, if you are subscribed to only one or two lists, it is best to send signoff messages directly to the LISTSERVs where your subscriptions are maintained.

Files on Demand

One fact about LISTSERV installations which may not be readily evident is their file server capability. The ability to distribute files of information upon request is built into LISTSERV. This capability allows LISTSERV to extend its functionality beyond its primary duty of supporting network mailing lists.

To find out what files are available from a particular LISTSERV installation, send it the INDEX command either via an interactive message or as the first line of a mail message. The LISTSERV will respond by sending a file called LISTSERV FILELIST. This file is usually a directory listing more filelists for various categories along with a short description of each of them. These filelists can be thought of as subdirectories which organize the files maintained on a LISTSERV into groups according to category. To acquire a particular file, send the command SENDME <filename> via an interactive or mail message, where <filename> is the name of the file you wish to retrieve.

LOCATING ELECTRONIC MAILING LISTS

The use of Wide Area Networks is affecting scholarship in many fields. In the early days of BITNET, most mailing list topics were computing oriented. This is no longer the case with the mailing lists that are being added today. New topics are as diverse as the scholarly fields of study and have included topic areas ranging from Hermann Hesse to Chinese poems. The number and variety of scholarly online discussion lists has obviously grown with geometric proportions.

With the number of lists growing, how is it possible to find a mailing list on a particular topic? That question may have a number of answers. One way to find out what lists are maintained on BITNET LISTSERVs is to send the command LIST GLOBAL to the nearest LISTSERV installation. One word of warning, however: this command will generate and send to you a file which is over 3,000 lines long. The lists are in alphabetical order, so if you are looking for the location of a list, this file can be very helpful. If, however, you are looking for mailing lists on your particular field of study, it could take a while to scan over 3000 entries. Fortunately, there is a way to scale down the list that is sent to you. If you are looking for a particular word or word fragment in a list name or description, you can send the LIST command as follows:

LIST GLOBAL /<string>

where <string> is the word or fragment for which you want to search. This will greatly narrow the number of entries in the file that is sent to you, however, since the list descriptions are very brief, it is possible that you will not find all lists on a particular topic.

There is an alternative source for finding BITNET and Internet mailing lists and discussion groups. Diane Kovacs, of the Kent State University Libraries, has compiled a directory of electronic mailing lists and news groups. The directory is actually a set of files which can be acquired from LISTSERV@KENTVM (and via anonymous FTP from KSUVXA.KENT.EDU in the library directory).

The files which make up the directory are as follows:
ACADLIST README   (explanatory notes for the Directory with an index)
ACADLIST FILE1   (Anthropology-Education)
ACADLIST FILE2   (Futurology-Latin American Studies)
ACADLIST FILE3   (Library and Information Science-Music)
ACADLIST FILE4   (Political Science-Writing)
ACADLIST FILE5   (biological sciences)
ACADLIST FILE6   (physical sciences)
ACADLIST FILE7   (business and general academia)
ACADLIST CHANGES   (all the major additions, deletions and alterations)

The organization of lists and news groups by subject allows easy access to those on one particular field of study. This is a obviously a valuable service to the Wide Area Network community of scholars.

Another very useful directory is one of electronic journals, compiled by Michael Strangelove at the University of Ottawa and available from LISTSERV@UOTTAWA as well as LISTSERV-@BROWNVM. It consists of two files, EJOURNL1 DIRECTRY and EJOURNL2 DIRECTRY, with entries organized by category of publication (journal, newsletter, digest, etc.). Each entry has the journal title, ISSN number (if any), a description, subscription information, submission information, related electronic mailing lists (if any), back issue information, and a contact name and address.

Mailing lists are being created on a daily basis and if it is your job to keep up with them, you may wish to subscribe to a mailing list whose sole purpose is to announce new lists. The list name is NEW-LIST@NDSUVM1, and to subscribe, send the following command (using the instructions above in "Using LISTSERV") to LISTSERV@NDSUVM1:

SUBSCRIBE NEW-LIST <your name>

There are also archives of this mailing list maintained on LISTSERV@NDSUVM1. You can send the command, SENDME NEW-LIST FILELIST, to LISTSERV@NDSUVM1 for a list of available archives. If you wish to inquire as to whether a list exists for a particular topic, you can send a message to the NEW-LIST mailing list. These inquiries are digested and distributed to the mailing list on a regular basis.

Another source of information on new mailing lists is the BITNET electronic magazine, NetMonth. NetMonth includes notices of new mailing lists and other information about BITNET and related networks. To subscribe to NetMonth send the command:

SUBSCRIBE NETMONTH <your name>,
to LISTSERV@MARIST.

DEFINING USENET

Ask networking experts to define USENET, and not only will you first get a perplexed look staring back at you, you may also get as many different answers as times that you ask the question. Because USENET is so wide spread and accessible by a number of networking technologies, it is easy to become bogged down in technical details when trying to get a grasp on USENET. For our purposes, let's ignore the technical part and concentrate on the content part.

USENET is a large collection of electronic mail messages that is distributed to many sites around the world. In order to keep all of this information accessible, it is organized into distinct topic areas called news groups. These news groups are organized hierarchically with the top-level hierarchies determining the overall nature of the content. For example, news groups in the "comp" hierarchy concentrate on computing-related issues, while news groups in the "soc" hierarchy discuss different cultures, societies, and social trends. Under each hierarchy, there are sub-groups and sub hierarchies. For example, comp.sys.amiga.hardware is a group devoted to discussing hardware issues related to Amiga computer systems, while soc.culture.indian offers news from India and discussions of social trends and current events in that country.

Not all news groups are maintained at all sites. In some areas there are even "local" news groups for a geographic or metropolitan area. Some of the more widely spread news group hierarchies are as follows:

> ALT—loosely moderated alternative discussions to the other more structured hierarchies;
> BIT—messages echoed from BITNET LISTSERV groups;
> COMP—computing and information system-related topics;
> K12—discussions related to and supporting Kindergarten-12th grade education;
> MISC—miscellaneous discussion topics;
> NEWS—discussions about USENET news;
> REC—"recreational" topics;
> SCI—discussions within scientific areas;
> SOC—social and cultural issues.

At your site, there may be more groups available than the ones listed above. It is possible find over 1,500 different USENET groups available at some installations.

USENET messages are usually accessed via specialized programs called news readers. A news reader program will establish contact with a computer system that maintains USENET messages and then oversees the transfer of the messages and their presentation to you. Since news readers work differently on different computing systems, you may need to contact your local system administrator for information about any news readers which may be available for your use.

Some news reader programs will allow you to "register" a subset of groups that you wish to read on a regular basis. This allows the news reader to present only the groups that you select, making it easier on a daily basis to find the discussions that most interest you. Considering the overwhelming number of discussions that are widely available, making use of a register feature within a news reader can save quite a bit of time.

E-MAIL GUIDELINES AND ETIQUETTE[2]

Back in the "old" days people were forced to perform their communication through writing, by hand, on blank sheets of paper and then conveying those blank sheets to others. It is even reported that the United States Postal Service, today known primarily for its ability to deliver multitudes of "junk mail" and bills to your door, conveyed large numbers of these hand-written communiques, known as "letters." The exchange of letters tended to foster a certain style of communication: letters were received and thoughtfully read; letters were generally more formal than spoken communication; letters had permanence and could be saved for later reference; in responding to letters, people would often think and then write one sentence, think and write another sentence, and so on. Today, electronic mail has revolutionized communication. There is no need for paper or messy handwriting utensils. You no longer have to use that formal writing style. Mail is received and read with heretofore unknown speed. It is now possible to dash off a reply to an electronic mail message without even thinking.

Well, maybe it's not quite that cut and dried, but electronic mail does seem to have the ability to evoke what are known in e-mail circles as "flames"—emotional responses to messages which don't necessarily do much to foster effective communication.

Norman Z. Shapiro and Robert H. Anderson, in a report prepared for the National Science Foundation and published by the Rand Corporation, list several possible causes for the flame phenomenon:

1. Difficulty in determining the formality of a message from its appearance;
2. Attempts at humor, irony, sarcasm, and wit are often misinterpreted;
3. Cues such as body language (or voice inflection) are lacking in electronic mail;
4. The ease of an immediate "reply" encourages "off the top of the head" responses;
5. Electronic messages containing hasty or ill-chosen words can stay in electronic in boxes or can be printed in a way that gives them importance never intended.[3]

Although anonymity is often mentioned as a factor, they observed no significant difference in "flaming" between remote correspondents who didn't know each other personally and those who did know each other.

Shapiro and Anderson go on to give several suggestions for minimizing the possible problems of "escalating emotions."

1. Carefully label messages that have a deliberate emotional content. Sometimes just the annotation "Flame! Flame!" alerts the reader to the fact that the writer knows he or she is being emotional.
2. Resist the temptation to fire off a response. Write the response, file it away, and wait 24 hours. Reconsider the response later, in the light of a new day (and perhaps a rereading and reinterpretation of the original message).
3. Use alternative media to break the cycle of message-and-response. A telephone call or personal conversation can do wonders, when we can use body language, eye contact, and the other cues we've developed. (Of course, this is not usually

possible in mailing list situations, but it is good advice regarding organizational electronic communication).

Just as in other human situations, the development of an etiquette can help solve some of the problems which potentially arise with electronic communication. John Quarterman, in his book entitled *The Matrix,*offers a number of suggestions concerning e-mail etiquette when sending messages to others or posting messages to BITNET LISTSERV or USENET mailing lists:

- Electronic mail is not like other media.   Treating e-mail just like the telephone, paper mail, or any other medium can lead to misunderstandings and mistakes.
- Emulate experienced users.   See how those already posting to mailing lists make the most effective use of those forums.
- Be brief.   Often a few well-chosen words are better than long-winded elaborations.
- Label your message.   Choose a title that fits the subject and stick to it.
- Remember your audience.   Use language, references, and subjects that will be comprehensible and not objectionable.
- Choose an appropriate medium and forum.   Use a conference or mailing list on a topic related to that of your message.
- Identify yourself.   Sign your message with some appropriate information such as your name and affiliation.
- Post new ideas.   Try not to repeat what has already been said except in brief confirmation.
- Respond to the topic and not the person.   Try to understand what the person is saying. If you can't understand what the person is saying, ask for a clarification. If you must criticize someone, give them a chance to respond. If you comment on the style of a message, respond to the content as well.
- Read other messages before responding.   Others may have already made the same obvious response.
- Don't respond in anger.   Wait a few minutes or hours, or even until the next day. If you are still angry when you respond, say so.

- Give the benefit of the doubt. Mistakes, misunderstand-ings, and ignorance are far more common than maliciousness.
- Be careful with humor and sarcasm. Many people have trouble recognizing these things even in person. Some networks have developed typographic conventions to get around the difficulties of expressing subtleties of expression through ASCII characters. One of the more universal is that UPPER CASE means shouting. Another is the use of the sideways "smiley face," :) or :-), to indicate lack of serious intent.
- Do be encouraging and polite. The most effective encourage-ment is often a simple response acknowledging a posting.
- Discourage when necessary. But do it privately and politely when possible. Don't discourage at all unless you're sure it's needed and that you are an appropriate one to do it.
- Assume permanence and ubiquity. Mail posted to discussion lists and sometimes even mail to individuals may be saved permanently, with or without your knowledge, and may be read by anyone, at any time, anywhere. Remember that even if a mail message has been deleted, it may exist somewhere on a backup tape.[4]

It's not enough just to observe etiquette. Quarterman also provides some valuable guidelines for e-mail ethics:

- Observe copyrights.
- Cite sources.
- Be careful with private correspondence. Do not redistribute private correspondence without permission. Don't read other people's mail without permission. If you receive a message by accident, return it to the sender or forward it to the intended recipient.
- Be honest. Don't distribute false information, and don't pretend to be someone you aren't in order to take unfair advantage of someone else.
- Someone is paying the bills. Remember that what you post may cost others time and money. Try to stick to useful information distributed to appropriate people.

- Don't post harmful instructions or information. Resource sharing systems are not like anything else. A computer network is neither like a home computer system nor like any other single computer system. The damage that can be caused by mistakes or malevolence increases with the power and extent of the system.[5]

Some of these points of etiquette or ethics are obvious; others, perhaps, wouldn't occur to you. By following these guidelines we can make electronic mail on BITNET or any other network a very effective and efficient means of communication. Or we can wax nostalgic for the good "old" days of paper, fountain pens, envelopes, stamps, and waiting five days to get a letter.

LIBRARY-RELATED MAILING LISTS AND DISCUSSION GROUPS

The following list of library related mailing lists was generated using the LIST GLOBAL/string command described above. This list is intended for illustrative purposes. A more comprehensive list of library-related mailing lists is regularly distributed on the PACS-L (PACS-L@UHUPVM1—Public-Access Computer Systems Forum) mailing list. This mailing list is an excellent one to read if you are interested in issues of computing as related to information sciences.

Name	Full address	List topic
Search string: BIB		
AIB-CUR	AIB-CUR@IVEUNCC	Discussione Associazione Italiana Biblioteche
BI-L	BI-L@BINGVMB	Bibliographic Instruction
KULHUM-L	KULHUM-L@UKANVM	KU Library Humanities Bibliographers
LIBMASTR	LIBMASTR@UOTTAWA	Library Master Bibliographic Database
LISRBC1L	LISRBC1L@NMSUVM1	ACRL Researh—Bibl. Control List1
LISRBC2L	LISRBC2L@NMSUVM1	ACRL Researh—Bibl. Control List2
PRO-CITE	PRO-CITE@IUBVM	PRO-CITE The Personal Bibliographic Software
Search string: CATALOG		

AUTOCAT	AUTOCAT@UVMVM	AUTOCAT: Library Cataloging and Authorities
INNOPAC	INNOPAC@MAINE	III Online Public Access Catalog
NOTRBCAT	NOTRBCAT@INDYCMS	Rare Book and Special Collections Catalogers

Search string: DOC

ARIE-L	ARIE-L@IDBSU	Discussion of the RLG Ariel Project
CONSALD	CONSALD@UTXVM	South Asian Libraries and Documentation
FLADOCS	FLADOCS@NERVM	Southeast Document Librarians
GOVDOC-L	GOVDOC-L@PSUVM	Discussion of Government Document Issues
JDOCS-DB	JDOCS-DB@TEMPLEVM	Journalism/Mass Comm Document Database
NCSUDDTP	NCSUDDTP@NCSUVM	NCSU Digitized Document Transmission Project

Search string: LIB

AFAS-L	AFAS-L@KENTVM	African American Studies and Librarianship
ALF-L	ALF-L@YORKVM1	Academic Librarian's Forum
ARCLIB-L	ARCLIB-L@IRLEARN	Irish and UK Architectural Libraries
ARLIS-L	ARLIS-L@UKCC	Art Libraries Society
ATLANTIS	ATLANTIS@HARVARDA	ATLANTIS—American Theological Library
BUSLIB-L	BUSLIB-L@IDBSU	Business Libraries
CALL-L	CALL-L@UNBVM1	Canadian Academic Law Libraries
CANST-LI	CANST-LI@UVMVM	CANST-LI: ACRL Canadian Studies Librarians
CIRCPLUS	CIRCPLUS@IDBSU	Library Circulation Issues
CIRLNET	CIRLNET@RUTVM1	Community of Industrial Relations Librarians
CONSALD	CONSALD@UTXVM	South Asian Libraries and Documentation
DLDG-L	DLDG-L@IUBVM	DLDG-L Dance Librarians
ELDNET-L	ELDNET-L@UIUCVMD	(ASEE) Engineering Libraries Division Network
ELLASBIB	ELLASBIB@GREARN	The Greek Library Automation System
EXLIBRIS	EXLIBRIS@RUTVM1	Rare Books and Special Collections
FISC-L	FISC-L@NDSUVM1	Fee-based Info. Serv. Centers in Acad. Orgs.
FLADOCS	FLADOCS@NERVM	Southeast Document Librarians
FLIPPER	FLIPPER@NERVM	Florida Librarians Interested in Preservation Programs
GEONET-L	GEONET-L@IUBVM	GEONET-L Geoscience Librarians & Information
GLSWICHE	GLSWICHE@ARIZVM1	Library Science
GSLIS-L	GSLIS-L@UTKVM1	Graduate School of Library and Information Science

.IP0,0/HARLIC-L	HARLIC-L@RICEVM1	HARLIC Libraries
HULINTRO	HULINTRO@HARVARDA	.IP0,0/HULINTRO—Harvard University Library Introduction
.IP0,0/ILL-L	ILL-L@UVMVM	Interlibrary Loan
INT-LAW	INT-LAW@UMINN1	.IP0,0/INT-LAW Foreign and International Law Issues for Librarians
.IP0,0/ITDHELP	ITDHELP@PURCCVM	Purdue Libraries
ITDSTAFF	ITDSTAFF@PURCCVM	Purdue Libraries
IULRES-L	IULRES-L@IUBVM	.IP0,0/Research Support for Indiana University Library
.IP0,0/JESSE	JESSE@ARIZVM1	Open Lib/Info Sci Education Forum
KATALIST	KATALIST@HUEARN	Discussion on librarian systems and databases
KUTUP-L	KUTUP-L@TRMETU	Turkish Libraries
LALA-L	LALA-L@UGA	Latin Americanist Librarians' Announcements
LIBADMIN	LIBADMIN@UMAB	Library Administration and Management
LIBALL	LIBALL@PURCCVM	Purdue Libraries
LIBEX-L	LIBEX-L@MAINE	Exhibits and Academic Libraries
LIBINFO	LIBINFO@HARVARDA	Harvard Library Information
LIBNET-L	LIBNET-L@NCSUVM	Libraries and Networks in North Carolina
LIBPER-L	LIBPER-L@KSUVM	Library Personnel Issues
LIBPLN-L	LIBPLN-L@QUCDN	University Library Planning
LIBRARY	LIBRARY@INDYCMS	Libraries & Librarians
LIBREF-L	LIBREF-L@KENTVM	Discussion of Library Reference Issues
LIBRES	LIBRES@KENTVM	Library and Information Science Research
LIBSCRN	LIBSCRN@PURCCVM	Purdue Libraries
LIBSYS	LIBSYS@UWAVM	LIBSYS
LIBTECH	LIBTECH@PURCCVM	Purdue Libraries
LM—NET	LM—NET@SUVM	School Library Media & Network Communications
MEDLIB-L	MEDLIB-L@UBVM	Medical Libraries
METALIB	METALIB@JPNTOHOK	Metallibrary
MITIRLIB	MITIRLIB@MITVMA	MIT Industrial Relations Library
MLA-L	MLA-L@IUBVM	Music Library Association
NOTMUS-L	NOTMUS-L@UBVM	NOTIS Music
OFFCAMP	OFFCAMP@WAYNEST1	Off-Campus Library Services
RLGLAW-L	RLGLAW-L@UMINN1	RLG Law Library
RLGLOC-L	RLGLOC-L@BINGVMB	RLG Library Systems Officer Forum
SERIALST	SERIALST@UVMVM	Serials in Libraries
SPILIB-L	SPILIB-L@SUVM	SPIRES
SUNYLA-L	SUNYLA-L@BINGVMB	SUNY Library Association
TESLA	TESLA@NERVM	Technical Standards for Library Automation
UBLIB-L	UBLIB-L@UBVM	UB Libraries

UNICRN-L	UNICRN-L@PSUORVM	SIRSI/UNICORN Automated Library Systems
UWREFLIB	UWREFLIB@UWAVM	UW Reference Library
VETLIB-L	VETLIB-L@VTVM2	Veterinary Medicine Library Issues and Information
VIRTUAL	VIRTUAL@INDYCMS	Library of the Future
WIML-L	WIML-L@IUBVM	Women's Issues in Music Librarianship

Search string: BRS, NOTIS, and VTLS

BRS-L	BRS-L@USCVM	BRS/Search Full Text Retrieval Software
IN-NOTIS	IN-NOTIS@IRISHVMA	Indiana NOTIS Sites and Users
INDNOTIS	INDNOTIS@INDYCMS	NOTIS Implementation in Indiana
NOTIS-L	NOTIS-L@TCSVM	NOTIS/DOBIS Discussion Group List
NOTISACQ	NOTISACQ@CUVMB	NOTIS Acquisitions Discussion Group
VTLSLIST	VTLSLIST@VTVM1	VTLS Users List

Search string: RESEARCH

ELEASAI	ELEASAI@ARIZVM1	Open Lib/Info Sci Research Forum
GTRTI-L	GTRTI-L@GSUVM1	Research & Teaching in Global Info Tech
LISRES-L	LISRES-L@NMSUVM1	ACRL Research—Expert Systems
LISRLE1L	LISRLE1L@NMSUVM1	ACRL Research—Library Effectiveness 1
LISRLE2L	LISRLE2L@NMSUVM1	ACRL Research—Library Effectiveness 2
LISRSC-L	LISRSC-L@NMSUVM1	ACRL Research—Scholarly Communication
LISRUU-L	LISRUU-L@NMSUVM1	ACRL Research—Understanding the User

Search string: Z39

| Z3950IW | Z3950IW@NERVM | Z39.50 Implementors Workshop |

NOTES

1. Editor's note: This chapter was written in July 1992.

2. Adapted from Philip Baczewski, "The BITNET Connection: Guidelines for Electronic Mail on BITNET (or Anywhere Else)." *Benchmarks* 12 (4):20 (April 1991).

3. Norman Z. Shapiro and Robert H. Anderson, "Toward an ethics and etiquette for electronic mail." Rand report number R-3283 (Rand, 1985).

4. John S. Quarterman, *The Matrix: Computer Networks and Conferencing Systems Worldwide* (Bedford, MA: Digital Press, 1990), p. 34.

5. Ibid.

ABOUT THE CONTRIBUTORS

Philip C. Baczewski is the Assistant Director of Academic Computing Services at the University of North Texas in Denton, Texas, where, among other things, he is the primary consultant for the BITNET and Internet wide area networks. He holds a Doctor of Musical Arts degree in music composition, and besides his networking activities, he continues to compose music and pursue research in music perception and cognition.

Billy Barron received his B.S. (1986) from North Texas State University and M.S. from the University of North Texas. He was recently appointed Network Services Manager of Academic Computing Services at the University of Texas at Dallas. Previously he was the VAX/UNIX Systems Manager at the University of North Texas. Mr. Barron has also worked for CICNet collecting electronic journals. He is heavily involved in networking and has compiled one of the major guides to library computer systems on the Internet.

Pauline S. Bayne is head of the George F. DeVine Music Library at the University of Tennessee, Knoxville. From 1990-1991 she co-directed a computer-based training development project at the University of Tennessee, working with a team of nine librarians. She continues to work with CBT for library staff and CAI for instruction of library users. She has published in the areas of music bibliography and managing the physical relocation of libraries.

Suzanne Bell was computer science librarian and online coordinator at Rochester Institute of Technology for four years. In September 1993 she became computer science librarian at Carnegie Mellon University. Ms. Bell has written about electronic systems in the Oxford (U.K.) College libraries for *Wilson Library Bulletin*. She has also written about effective liaison with computer scientists for the Special Libraries Association Annual Conference. She is a charter member of the A.C.M.'s Librarians Advisory Group.

Susan P. Besemer is Director of Reed Library at SUNY College, Fredonia. She holds an M.L.S. From Indiana University (1967), M.S. in Creative Studies from Buffalo State College (1980), and an advanced studies certificate in Information and Library Studies from SUNY Buffalo (1988). Author of *From Museums, Galleries, and Studios: A Guide to Artists on Film and Tape* (Greenwood Press), Ms. Besemer does creative problem solving training for organizations and empirical research in creativity studies.

Linda Coppola is the Humanities/Social Sciences Reference Librarian at Rochester Institute of Technology. She was involved in the initial selections for the electronic journals collection and offered basic instruction for their use through the library's seminar series. Linda is active in the Western New York/Ontario chapter of ACRL and the RIT Women's Network. She has done extensive bibliographic instruction and attended many workshops in that area.

Maryruth Phelps Glogowski received her B.A. in English and her M.L.S. from the State University of New York at Buffalo. She is currently the Interim Director at the Edward H. Butler Library at Buffalo State College. She is the author of the *Management Media Directory* and has done research with Dr. Neil Yerkey applying cluster analysis to the scatter of information science literature under a grant from The Council on Library Resources. Maryruth has also administered two multi-institutional grants for staff development series.

Linda Marie Golian began her library career at the University of Miami in Coral Gables, Florida and is currently the Serials Librarian at Florida Atlantic University. She received her M.L.S. from Florida State University and is now enrolled in the Ed.D. program specializing in adult education.

Taylor E. Hubbard has been on the faculty of Evergreen State College since 1986 as a reference librarian and member of the teaching faculty, combining collection development in social sciences and reference duties with teaching law, history and the sociology of knowledge. His publications and papers include aspects of information technology use and policy and topics related to the sociology of information organization. He is a graduate of the University of Vermont, San Francisco State University and UCLA and has held professional positions at universities in Alaska, Colorado and New York.

Tessa Killian was the Serials/Reference Librarian at the Olive Kettering Library, Antioch College, Yellow Springs, Ohio. She received her B.A. from the State University of New York College at Fredonia and her M.L.S. from the State University of New York at Buffalo.

Lynn K. Milet is the Director of Instructional Media Services and Associate Director of Libraries at Lehigh University. She holds an Ed.D. in educational technology from Lehigh University, an M.L.S. from the State University of New York, Geneseo, and an M.S. in biology and an M.Ed. in secondary education from the University of Bridgeport, Bridgeport, CT. She is also an adjunct faculty member in the Lehigh University Graduate School of Education and Allentown College of St. Francis DeSalles. In addition to these activities, Dr. Milet is a consultant to various businesses, private industry, and other organizations in the use and implementation of instructional technology for training and education. She currently serves on the Board of Directors of the Association of Educational Communications and Technology and will assume the position of President-elect in February, 1994.

Marilyn Nelson holds the M.L.S. from the State University of New York at Buffalo where she is currently a candidate for the Ph.D. in Social Foundations in the Graduate School of Education's Organization, Administration and Policy Department. The topic of her research is "Librarianship's Feminist Evolution in the Harlem Renaissance Ethos."

Jean M. Purnell was appointed Dean of Libraries and Director of Audio-Visual Services at the University of the Pacific in Stockton, California in 1992. She has also served as Music Librarian and as a manager of both public and technical services departments since her initial appointment in 1984. She holds a B.A. from Wake Forest University and an M.A. in Musicology and an M.L.S. from the University of North Carolina at Chapel Hill. Ms. Purnell's professional interests include human resources management, planning and organizational performance measures, and development of music and audio-visual collections and facilities.

Carol J. Richards is Coordinator of Information and Access Services at E.H. Butler Library at Buffalo State College where she holds the faculty rank of Librarian. She has been employed at Butler Library continuously since 1974, serving at various times as Reference Librarian, Library Instruction Coordinator, and Head of Information Services. Training new staff is an ongoing activity.

Peter Scott is the Manager of Small Systems at the University of Saskatchewan Libraries in Canada. He is the author of *HYTELNET: Hypertext Guide to Internet Resources*. Mr. Scott is also a frequent speaker at networking conferences. He was recently chosen to receive the Meckler Research and Education Networking Award.

Kristin Senecal "crossed the divide" and learned the art and science of cataloging after six year of working as a reference librarian in academic libraries. She was pleased to discover that she enjoyed it, but what surprised her was how cataloging enhanced her abilities in reference. She is currently head of Technical Services at Spahr Library, but still puts in her hours on the reference desk and loves being able to practice her profession as both a technical and public service librarian.

Sara B. Sluss has been a reference librarian at Baruch College since 1985 and has been Associate Librarian for Reader Services since 1990. Professor Sluss has also published articles in *Book Research Quarterly, Urban Academic Librarian, The Reference Librarian,* and *Library Journal.*

Joanna M. Walsh is Principal of Walsh Associates, a library consulting firm founded in 1982. She is also Adjunct Professor at the University of Rhode Island Graduate School of Library and Information Science. She has prepared training plans and planned and presented numerous training programs. Ms. Walsh was the Coordinator of the Boston Library Consortium and has held several positions in academic libraries. She holds and M.S. in library Science from Simmons College School of Library and Information Science and an M.A. in History from Northeastern University.

Margaret R. Wells is Director of the Oscar A. Silverman Undergraduate Library at the University at Buffalo, State University of New York, where she was previously Head of the Instruction Program and organized staff training for the online system of the University Libraries. She holds an M.L.S. from the University at Buffalo and a B.A. from the University of Notre Dame. She has presented many workshops and published articles in *Research Strategies.* She is also active in the Bibliographic Instruction Section of the American Library Association/ Association of College and Research Libraries.

Linda Lou Wiler, a graduate of UCLA Graduate School of Library Science, has worked with volunteers throughout her career in public and technical services. Her work at the Chicago Public Library gave her excellent training in staff development and organization. At Florida Atlantic University, where she is currently employed as development officer for the library, she started the volunteer program in the early eighties.

AUTHOR INDEX

SUBJECT INDEX

AACR2 96, 98, 108, 112
Activities 8, 14, 18, 28, 29, 31, 35, 36, 39, 43, 46, 92, 93, 115, 150, 152, 154, 158, 165, 168, 179
America's Choice: High Skills or Low Wages! 55, 69
Anglo-American Cataloging Rules 96, 108
Antioch College 21, 27
Apple Computer, Inc. 5, 20
Application form 38, 41
Archenstone PC 179
Archiving 186, 188
Automation 2, 10, 35, 55, 56, 58, 59, 64-66, 68, 71, 82, 83, 87, 88, 92, 107, 184, 191, 192, 222, 223
BI 168, 189, 221
Bibliographic instruction 22, 24, 160, 165, 167, 168, 221
Biological Abstracts 164
BISON 72-74, 77
BITNET 20, 175, 176, 178, 191, 196, 200, 201, 207-216, 219, 221, 224
BLEND 175, 176, 190
BRS 141, 175, 224

CAI 6, 94
Cataloging Service Bulletin 97
CBT 6, 7, 9, 11, 13-19, 61
CD-ROM 22, 33, 43, 55, 139-141, 143, 144, 153, 176, 186
Checklist 15, 27-32
Chemical Abstracts 33, 164
City University of New York 141
Cleveland State 123
Communication 2, 19, 47, 51, 58, 76, 88, 89, 100, 107, 151, 177, 179, 188, 192, 208, 217-219, 221, 224
Computer-assisted instruction 6, 94
Computer-assisted learning 6
Computer-based training 5-7, 15, 17, 19, 61, 62
Connecting 19, 177, 194, 196-198, 202, 204
Contents note 60, 104-106, 182
CPS 129, 132
Creative problem solving 1, 20, 33, 36, 110, 123-130, 132-137
Creativity 44, 81, 92, 123-130, 133, 135, 136
Creativity training 130
CUNY 144, 146, 147